THE COLLECTOR'S BOOK OF

# DOLLS

THE COLLECTOR'S BOOK OF

# DOLLS

CHARTWELL
BOOKS, INC.

BRENDA GERWAT-CLARK

# DEDICATED TO

My parents where it all began — for saving my old childhood dolls; to my husband, Stephen, for starting me on this consuming hobby and sharing it with me over the years; to my daughters Naomi and Leona for their patient understanding; to Tesse for working with me on my dolls and for her wonderful costumes, and to my friends who have made a silent yet no less important contribution.

A QUINTET BOOK

Published by Chartwell Books
A Division of Book Sales, Inc.
110 Enterprise Avenue
Secaucus, New Jersey 07094



ISBN 1 55521 070 8

This book was designed and produced by
Quintet Publishing Limited
6 Blundell Street London N7

Art Director: Peter Bridgewater
Editor: Josephine Bacon
Photographer: Michael Freeman

Typeset in Great Britain by
Central Southern Typesetters, Eastbourne
Manufactured in Hong Kong by
Regent Publishing Services Limited
Printed in Hong Kong by
Leefung-Asco Printers Limited

COVER:

FROM LEFT, TOP TO BOTTOM

*1 German character doll, the head marked "K * R 117".*
*2 French Bru Jne. bébé doll, the head marked '9'.*
*3 Eden bébé, another French doll.*
*4 A French A-mould Steiner open-mouth doll.*
*5 German Simon & Halbig doll.*
*6 Early German Belton-head type doll with closed mouth.*

# CONTENTS

# INTRODUCTION

This book is written firstly to whet the appetite of the would-be antique doll collector and to inspire her (or his) imagination. I say 'his' in this way because, contrary to popular belief, very many men, young and old, collect dolls. The book aims to assist the collector, once inspired in discovering just how and where to begin and how to avoid making costly mistakes, and to give guidance on what to collect. When I first began to collect dolls, there was practically no literature available apart from one or two out-of-print books on the library shelves which were not very helpful. In those days you learned by every costly mistake you made.

In your search for knowledge in your hobby you will sometimes find inconsistencies in various areas. Much of the knowledge has been pieced together relatively recently in historical terms. Doll factories generally did not keep archives, and knowledge of what they made previously was usually not recorded by the companies themselves; as living memory died, the details were lost. Much information is found only in old patent registers, and searching through them gives us clues as to how things were made and when they date from, but factory marks on heads have been laboriously recorded by collectors and doll historians. Sometimes we can only suggest a date of manufacture by a certain company through knowing roughly the period during which it operated from a specific address. Vague it may be sometimes, but it suffices to spur the true enthusiast in the quest for knowledge and each clue, however small, may be vital in piecing together a whole body of information. Sometimes an old newspaper stuffed into the doll's head when new has proved to be the only evidence as to a doll's date of manufacture.

Doll-collecting terms, such as wax dolls, wooden, bisque, papier mâché, china and so on, rarely refer to the whole doll, that is, body, arms and legs. The reference is only to the head. When we want to describe the whole doll as being of any particular material we term it an 'all bisque doll' or 'all china doll', for example. 'Open' and 'closed' mouth doll refers exactly to that. The closed mouth dolls are more rare and costly; the open mouths were generally made at a later date and examples will have teeth.

RIGHT Left *Pale bisque shoulder plate doll with closed mouth, delicate face painting and eyebrows and a solid dome Belton-type head. The doll appears to be unmarked but may be marked under the leather body. She has bisque arms and an early kid body and kid feet with stitched toes. She wears an original two-piece dress and matching bonnet. (Author's collection).* Right *Good-quality closed-mouth shoulder plate doll, 50cm/20in tall, dressed as a young man with solid domed Belton-type head, turned to one side. He has a kid body and an unmarked head. He has bisque arms, early gusseted kid body and original suit, shirt, waistcoat and top hat. He is probably an early Kestner. (Author's collection).*

The art of the doll has been with us for thousands of years. Early wood or stone figures in human form would later have given way to cloth or rag in some shape. Very ancient dolls were used for ritual or sacrifice, and the concept of the doll as a child's plaything is a later derivative of this.

Man's obvious need for such objects is deep rooted and goes back to early times. The doll is an object of love and of beauty, cherished from childhood, the keeper of secrets. It is also an historical record of past fashions and craftsmanship. Dolls can be regarded as an important form of folk art, bringing together the skills of the designer and craftsman, with the technological knowhow and the materials of the age. They are then expressed in art forms, portraits of characters from fiction and everyday life, or movie characters such as Charles Chaplin and so on. They are an expression of an age, encompassing fashion and popular trends, and give us a charming and informative view of the past with all its dreams and aspirations.

The child remains in us all, and although it may become buried deep through years and wisdom, the magic which draws us inquiringly to this art form is the same magic which inspires some half million other adults throughout the world to collect dolls. In doll collecting you are indeed embarking on a very rewarding, exciting and sometimes frustrating hobby, time-consuming perhaps — for some all-consuming — but certainly an experience not to be missed. You are joining a worldwide family of other collectors and enthusiasts who will impart to you their knowledge and friendship, sharing with you their collections and accompanying you on the hunt. For a hunt it will certainly be. If only our dolls could talk, what stories they would have to tell.

Your life will never be the same again, and as these cherished little folk creep slowly into your life, filling up your chairs, your china cabinet and your sofa, you will realize that you are now the curator of your own private museum and that the dolls have come down to us from other childhoods

FAR LEFT Left *Open-mouthed character baby doll, head marked '996 A & M', 22.5cm/9in with bent limb composition body and original clothes. (Naomi Gerwat-Clark's collection).* Right *Closed-mouth Kestner character doll with intaglio eyes, painted brush-stroke hair and bent limb baby body, head marked '142'. (Courtesy Granny's Goodies).*

OPPOSITE *The larger doll is a Victorian shop model, 125 cm/50 in high, with poured wax, removable head. She has glass eyes, real hair wig and her eyelashes and eyebrows are rooted into the head. The wooden body has fully articulated arms, stained brown, and poured wax hands. The wooden legs are straight. The costume is original (Author's collection). In the perambulator (baby buggy), she has a bisque-headed, open-mouth Armand Marseille 'Dream Baby' doll, marked A.M. 351/8K. The body is composition bent limb. (Chelsea Lion Collection).*

LEFT *Early child's play doll in woven textile from Peru, 1st century A.D. and recovered from a child's tomb. The limbs may be modern replacements. (Granny's Goodies - London).*

long ago, just as we will pass them on. Love them as you may, restore them only when necessary but do, please, remember to keep them in as near original condition as possible, for they are records not of our present, but of our past.

## WHERE TO START

**BOOKS** It cannot be stressed too strongly, that there is only one way to begin doll collecting, and that is to read, read and read. Do not skimp in this direction and do not skimp on the money you invest in your books, for they will be your chief source of information and will be a constant source of reference when you are in doubt about something you might want to buy. All too often novice collectors make a first purchase in a rush and then discover their bargain item was not such a bargain after all. Start with more general books and encyclopaedias before purchasing in-depth studies on certain types of dolls or manufacturers, but do build a good library. Books will certainly save you a lot of money in the long run. Most do not stay on the shelves for ever — many have fairly short runs — so when a good book comes out buy it and build your library.

**AUCTIONS** Get the experience of handling dolls yourself. At auctions, for example, you can (carefully) handle dolls at the viewing prior to the sale. Remember, if you break one you will probably find you have bought it! A word of caution here: auctions are for professionals or experienced collectors and can be a risk to the newcomer. If you make the final bid then you must buy — there is no changing your mind. As a novice collector, beware of auction houses which do not tell you the condition of each doll in their catalogue, and never buy a doll at auction unless you have viewed the items for sale very carefully. Ascertain also if there is a buyer's premium to be added to the final bid price of the doll.

**DOLL FAIRS** Doll Fairs provide a good opportunity for inspecting a lot of dolls and meeting dealers. You may even meet a dealer from your own area who could be very helpful. There are doll fairs up and down the country and dates and venues are generally published in specialist magazines.

**MUSEUMS** Now that doll collecting has gained in status, several museums have formed collections devoted exclusively to dolls and toys, and there are many more with a good doll section. It is important to visit the doll museums and travelling exhibitions up and down the country and look at as many different types of dolls as you can. Museums obviously give you a wide range of dolls with which to become acquainted.

**FLEA MARKETS OR GENERAL MARKETS** Beware, too, of the so called 'bargain' at the flea market. You may be lucky enough to find a rare doll for a small price, but the chances are very slight and you may also be purchasing a reproduction unknowingly as there will be no guarantees unless you are buying from a specialist. You may at the same time be buying a cracked or damaged doll or a marriage of various doll parts, all of which will significantly affect the value, should you wish to sell the doll later.

**DEALERS** Dealers are by far the best sources for the new collector. Find a reputable doll dealer whom you can trust and who is ready to give friendly and helpful advice. Most dealers are ready to do just that. In the quiet atmosphere of a doll shop you are free to browse and ask for advice on purchases, and perhaps even at some later date you will be able to sell your doll back to the dealer as a trade-in on a more valuable one. There are no snap decisions to be made. A good dealer can help you to build your collection wisely. After all, you are also buying his or her knowledge and years of experience and this is invaluable if one day you wish to resell some dolls in your collection or to upgrade it. A good dealer will ultimately save you money by helping you not to make a mistake. Because he has his name and reputation at stake he will want to give you sound advice. Most people would rarely buy stocks and shares without the advice of a stockbroker, so unless you have the experience yourself, take the advice of your doll broker.

# WOODEN DOLLS

Wood was used as a material for doll making because it was inexpensive. In the 17th and 18th centuries the main areas for wood carving were the Grödner Tal in the Austrian Tyrol, Bavaria, and Thuringia in Germany. Obviously these densely-wooded areas provided the ideal conditions for a wood-carving-based industry and it is not difficult to understand why such an industry thrived in this period. Wooden dolls were also carved in France and England. In a British will of 1548 a wooden-headed doll covered with plaster is mentioned, and the manufacture of wooden babies on a lathe is documented as early as 1733 in England.

St. Ulrich, the main town in the Grödner Tal in Austria was the centre of a toy industry which had existed since the early 18th century. The region was deeply religious, heavily wooded and remote, and it is easy to see how the early carved religious figures in the churches became the models for locally-made dolls. There would have been a natural progression from carved religious figures to children's dolls to be sold in the markets. The people of the area led an isolated life high in the Alps, snowed up in winter, with no other work, until about 1856 when access to the area became easier. Apart from dolls, carved animals of ash, pear and boxwood, turned on a lathe, were produced.

## MANUFACTURE

As far as the manufacture of wooden dolls is concerned we know only what we see: no patents existed and a great deal of modern detective work has resulted only in limited knowledge about who made the dolls and in what quantities. From a knowledge of the period's social history and economics as well as from articles and family histories we begin to build a picture of these dolls which have been such a mystery to us for so long. An article written in 1875 describes how wooden dolls were painted by outworkers who earned a farthing a dozen, out of which paint and size had to be bought. If they worked full time, they could paint several hundred dozen per week, which seems an enormous output. Whole families, particularly in the isolated areas such as Grödner Tal, would be engaged in this work, some carving the dolls and

LEFT *Wooden Queen Anne-type doll, 52.5 cm/21 in tall with black pupilless enamel eyes and stitched eyebrows. The gesso-covered head is in good condition with tiny painted mouth and rouged cheeks. The, stump-type, one-piece body has jointed, painted wooden limbs, wig base nailed to the head (early 19th century). (Author's collection).*

others painting them. The guilds were quite strong at the time — the continental guilds being stronger than the English — and there was strict demarcation between carvers and painters.

A different stage in the painting would be undertaken each day, to allow drying time in between. When finished, the dolls were sold by pedlars who would travel the length and breadth of the land, and indeed other lands, selling their wares. The pedlars would visit Bohemia or Saxony to obtain their dolls encouraging foreign trade and a thriving industry.

Who were these carvers who made such priceless treasures, following a similar style? They may have belonged to a school of artisans who learned from a single master craftsman and then, having developed techniques for using certain materials, they followed tradition. Or they may have been individual craftsmen working independently throughout the country from lathes in their own tiny workrooms and in their own particular styles which coincidentally had numerous similarities.

BELOW *A rare collection of early wooden dolls, part of a 22-piece university graduation ceremony representing all the different faculties taking part. All the dolls are wooden Grödnertal dolls with fully articulated jointed wooden bodies, delicately-painted faces and fine hair detail, 13.75 cm/5½ in tall, and all in the completely original state. (Author's collection).*

## 'QUEEN ANNE' DOLLS AND 'QUEEN ANNE TYPES'

Among the most sought after wooden dolls are the so-called 'Queen Anne' dolls, or 'Queen Anne Type' dolls. In fact some of these pre-date Queen Anne (who ruled between 1702 and 1714), and

others were made well into the 19th century. They are associated with England and although examples are quite often found in the USA they were probably taken there by the early settlers. It is fairly certain that the Queen Anne type doll had its birth and adolescence in England.

These dolls had bodies turned on a lathe, with hand-carved heads and painted eyes or black, pupilless enamelled eyes; sometimes the eyes were blue. The head and body was carved from one piece of wood to form a stump, and the head was finished with gesso and varnish and delicate face painting. The fingers and hands were finely carved and gesso-covered and attached to the body with cloth and a pin. The legs were carved and jointed and set into grooves at the base of the torso; they often had well-defined calves and ankles. The eyebrows on the earlier dolls were the socalled 'stitched' variety, produced by a series of little black dots. The dolls were made with a high breast form, obviously to give a better line to the clothes of the period. The actual torso was left unfinished. The wig was tacked or nailed on to the head, and sometimes a black 'patch' was evident on the cheek — then considered a sign of beauty.

The styles did, in fact, change through the decades. It may have been a case of detail giving way in the face of mass production, or it may have been simply a change of technique which altered their look. The later dolls are less realistic than the

earlier ones and appear to lack the craftsmanship. Their faces are of moulded plaster on a simple wooden stump, which would have been a cheaper process than the laborious hand carving of the earlier dolls.

## Peg Woodens Or Dutch Dolls

ABOVE *Wooden Queen Anne-type doll dating from 1850, with gesso-covered head, black pupilless enamel eyes, small painted lips, highly-rouged cheeks, jointed wooden limbs with lower section painted white, painted green boots and real hair wig. (Granny's Goodies - London).*

The so called 'Peg Wooden' or 'Dutch doll' was not, in fact, Dutch, nor was it a derivative of Deutsch, but it came from Austria. At the beginning of the 19th century we have the doll with elongated body, spoon-like, gesso-covered hands, jointed hips and knees, gesso-covered lower legs and painted slippers, usually of orange or deep pink. These dolls are also known as 'Penny Woodens' and 'Nürnberg Filles' and they come from the Bavarian and Austrian Tyrol. The carving of the head and body is usually refined and the face painting is subtle, suggesting care and skill in the making rather than a cheap plaything quickly turned out. The painting of the hair is also exceptional, with a multitude of tiny painted curls setting a frame for the face. The dolls come in a whole range of sizes from 15 cm/6 in up to 60 cm/24 in. Some exceptionally small examples exist, a few even fitting into a walnut. Some were made with a carved comb on the head and this was almost always painted yellow. The name 'tuck comb

RIGHT *Late peg wooden doll, 55 cm/22 in with crude face painting, fully jointed body and crudely-painted lower arms and legs ending in stumps. She is extremely well dressed in period clothing, which is not original. (Author's collection).*

woodens' has been lovingly given by collectors to this type of doll which was manufactured, with variations, for 50 years, making dating difficult.

By the end of the 19th century Dutch dolls had taken on an entirely different character. The delicate face painting and structure of the earlier dolls were gone. To meet the needs of mass production and a wider buying public, a doll was developed with a solid head, shaped rather like the knob on a naval port. The painting was extremely crude, with black hair, dots for features and red blobs for cheeks. The head and body were still formed from a single piece of wood, but the torso was much shorter than that of the earlier dolls; the arms and legs were rudimentary, the hands being without detail and spoon-shaped, articulated at the elbow.

## Pedlar Dolls

It was a popular habit to turn peg wooden dolls into pedlar dolls with tiny trays or baskets displaying a multitude of wares for sale. An original collection can form a fascinating social record of the life and times of a particular doll, as many pedlars would carry all kinds of wares from cottons, pots and pans and sewing equipment, to purses, pictures, ornaments and religious items. Sometimes, the pedlar trays are not contemporary with the doll. It is quite easy to detect a tray recently put together, even for the inexperienced, as everything will appear newly-arranged and probably the glue will be visible. Both male and female pedlars are found, some covered with glass domes to protect them from dust.

## Wooden Schoenhut Dolls

The name of Schoenhut first comes to mind when thinking of later wooden dolls (see American Dolls page 79). Albert Schoenhut was born in 1850 in Germany and went to America when he was 17 years old. His wooden Humpty Dumpty Circus is perhaps his best loved creation, but the Schoenhut wooden dolls have a singular appeal in that they can be positioned rather like artists' mannequins and their faces are gentle and whimsical.

## Collecting Wooden Dolls – Where To Begin

Early wooden dolls are not for the collector with a limited budget: early examples tend to be highly priced and are generally in the top range of dolls in terms of value. However, the Schoenhut dolls would probably belong in the middle range, being later and a little more easily available, at least in America. 19th and early 20th-century peg woodens can be found at the lower end of the price range.

# CHINA DOLLS

China-headed dolls, made from hard-paste porcelain, with their high glaze and fascinating hairstyles are an exciting area of collecting, providing great social history interest and wide variety for the collector.

As with papier mâché dolls (see page 39) heads were often sold alone for the bodies to be made by mothers or nursemaids. China heads on their own are quite commonly found and are now extremely collectable. Most chinas are unmarked. The word 'chinas' is a collector's abbreviation for 'china-headed dolls,' and if one is found with a mark this is regarded as a real bonus.

Chinas were produced from around 1830, and represented men, women and children in glazed porcelain. Production continued well into the 1900's, and yet knowledge of chinas is scant, which makes dating a tantalizingly difficult task.

BELOW *Early China pink lustre shoulder head doll, 15 cm/6 in, unmarked and with brown moulded ringlets hanging straight down with extremely fine detail. The head probably dates around 1840.*

OVERLEAF *Four shoulder china dolls' heads with black painted hair.* left to right *10 cm/4 in shoulder head with 2 sew holes, 'low-brow' style hair, blue painted eyes, red eyelid line (1890); 10 cm/4 in head with 3 sew holes and unusual hair style taken back behind the ears (1880); 12.5 cm/5 in shoulder head with 3 sew holes, 24 moulded ringlets around the head, otherwise simple style, well-defined face painting and highly-rouged cheeks, and red eyelid line (1860-70); 10 cm/4 in shoulder head, with 2 sew holes, deeply sloping shoulders, 10 moulded ringlets and heavily-rouged cheeks (1860-70). (Author's collection).*

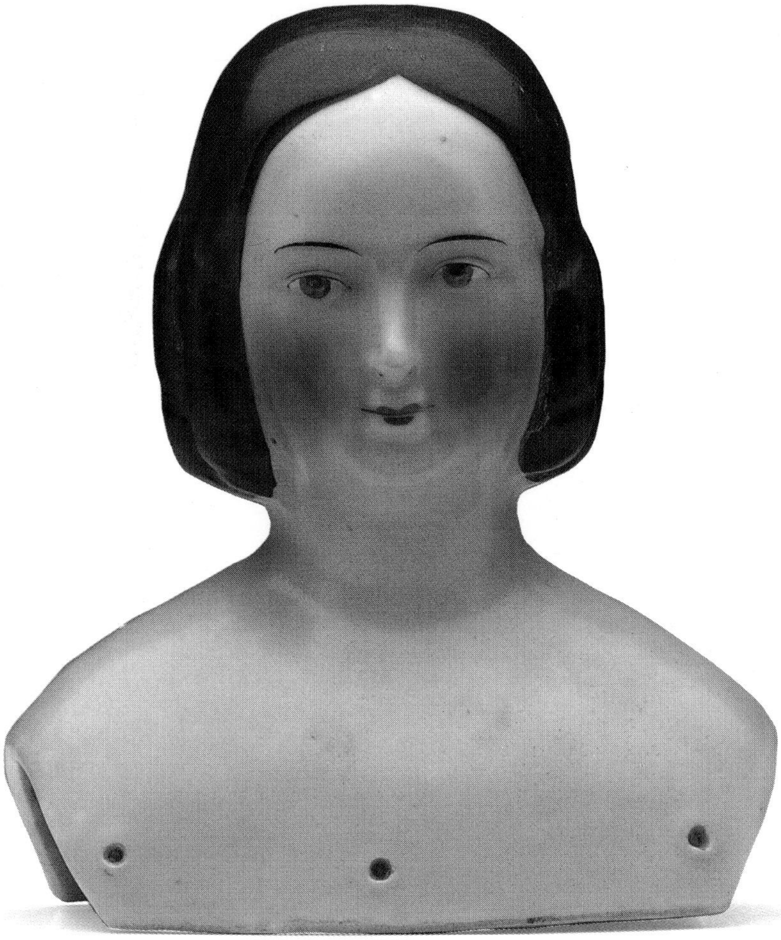

## BODIES

As the chinas could be purchased as heads only and the bodies would then have been made at home, many are found on very crude bodies, varying in shape as much as the skills of the loving hands that made them. Other chinas are found on commercially-made peg-wooden jointed bodies with china limbs jointed at elbows and knees. These tend to be amongst the most rare bodies on chinas. Some chinas are found on commercially-made rigid leather bodies with leather arms and hands: these are so stiff that most cannot be arranged in a seated position. These are often the bodies found on the earlier dolls. Commercial cloth bodies may also be found on some dolls, and these have china arms with well-defined fingers and china legs with painted black boots, and garter ribbons with bows usually painted in pink. Not all boots are painted black — they have been found in a variety of colours, including orange and

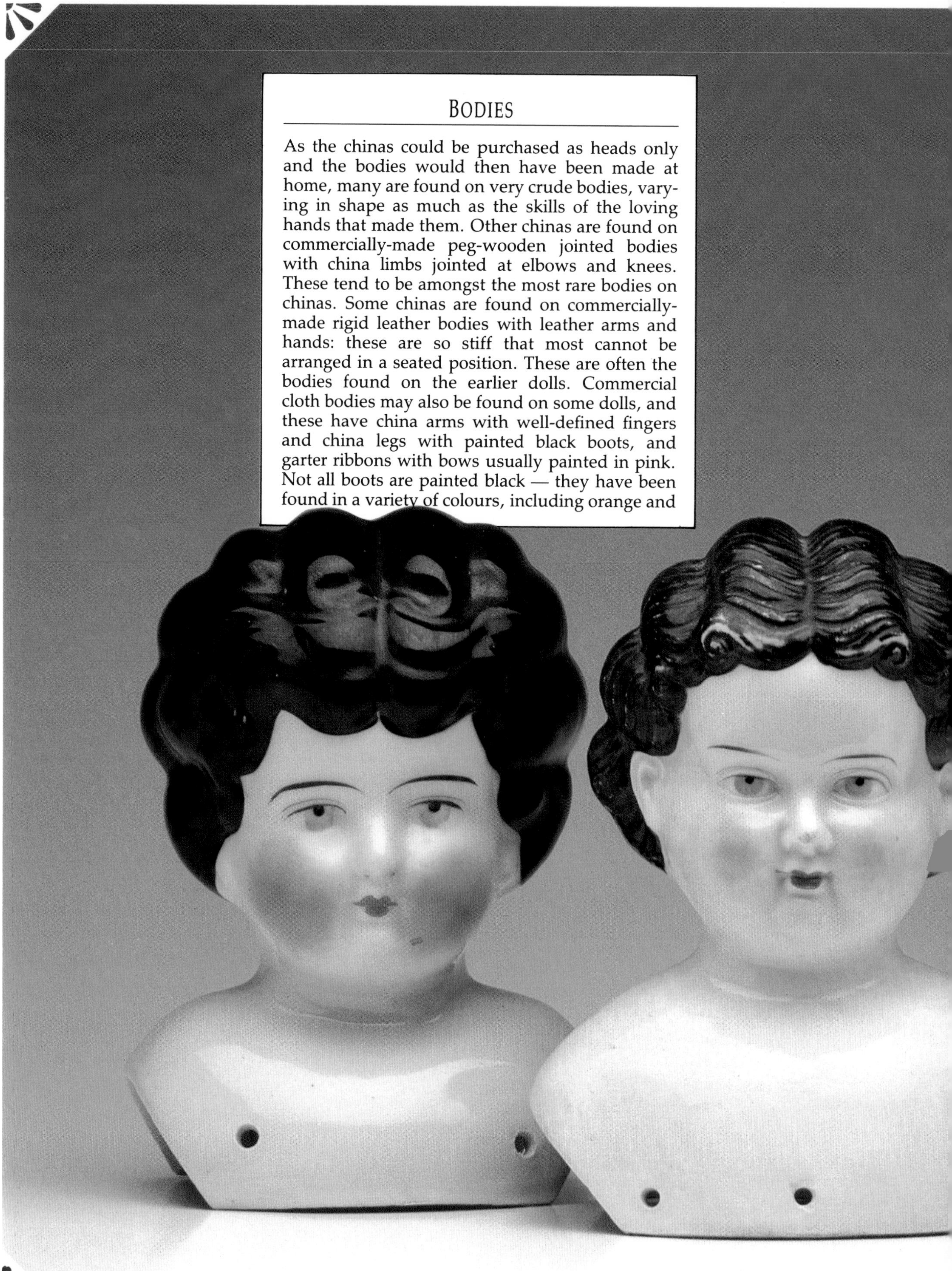

purple lustre. The collector who has found a good china head and who wishes to make it into a doll can make her (or his) own, at least until an old body can be found.

## MANUFACTURE OF 'CHINAS'

Most heads were made by pouring liquid clay into moulds. Another method was to press rolled-out clay into moulds. Poured heads are fairly smooth inside, while pressed heads are uneven. Some chinas are referred to by collectors as 'pink lustre' heads and these deeply-coloured examples are most desirable. The so-called pink lustre is a pink enamel glaze, obtained by applying a film of gold over the rose colour of the head. Generally the deeper lustres are earlier, the later ones tending to be paler. There are, of course, exceptions to every rule and pink lustre was made up until the 1900s. The heads were attached to the cloth bodies by

gluing, by stitching through the sew holes (the holes made by the manufacturer at the lower edge of the shoulder plate), or by nailing through the sew holes. These holes are generally considered to be an indication of the age of the doll, and most collectors are of the opinion that chinas with three sew holes at the base are among the earlier examples. However, some chinas have three holes in the front and two at the back which confounds this theory, but there may have been a need for three sew holes because of the slope at the base of the shoulder plate. Some early dolls have also been found with four sew holes. It should be pointed out that once a mould was made, if it was a popular seller, it probably remained in continuous use over a long period: for example, a particular doll, first made in 1850, might still have been in production in 1865 — yet another reason why accurate dating is so difficult.

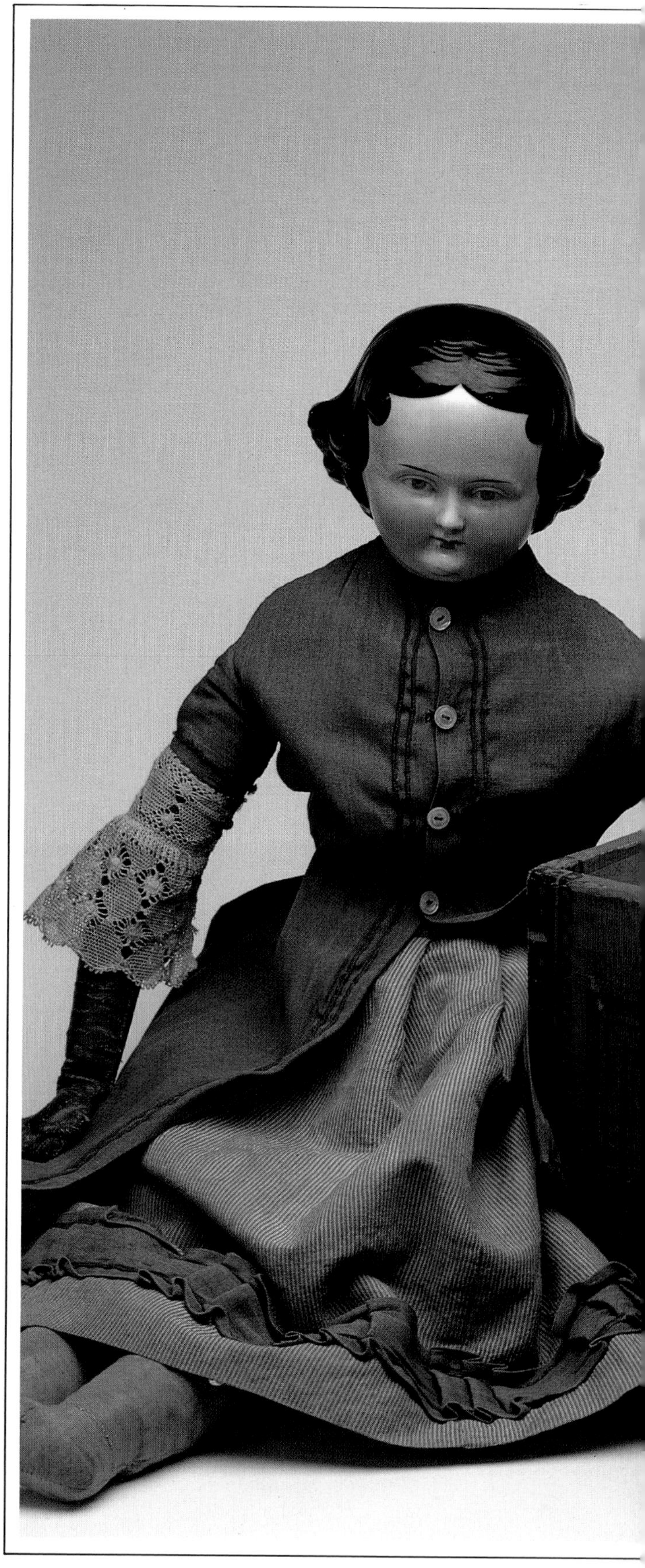

RIGHT *Pink lustre shoulder plate china-headed doll, 65 cm/26 in tall, on Lacmann-type body with long legs, red leather arms and well-detailed hands. She wears her original clothes. The head has soft curls over the ears, red eyeliner, and sloping shoulders with three sew holes front and back, 1860. (Author's collection).*

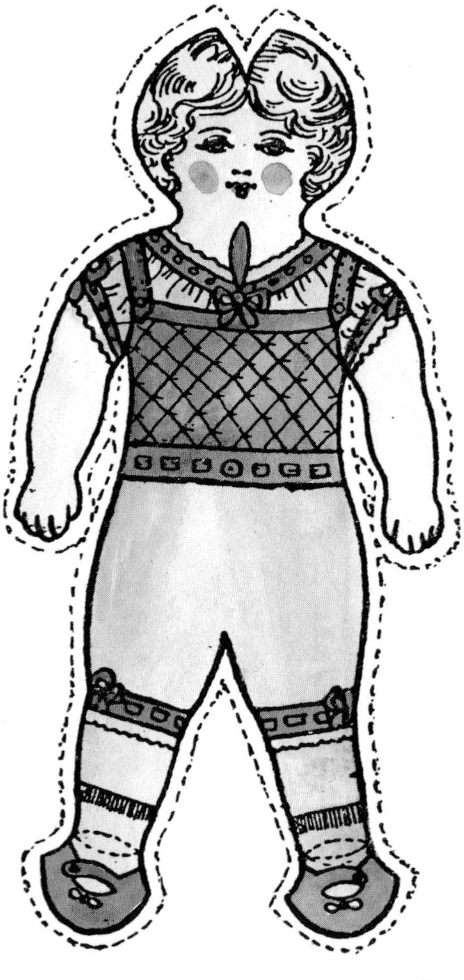

## GERMAN AND DANISH CHINAS

Some of the renowned porcelain factories of the first half of the 19th century, such as Meissen, Royal Copenhagen and Königliche Porzellan Manufaktur (KPM) in Berlin, made china-headed dolls, and there were many others, mostly producing unmarked examples. The quality of modelling, painting and craftsmanship in these early dolls is outstanding. They usually had brown or black painted hair, painted eyes and a pink lustre to the china which gives a warmth to the skin tones. Later Chinas had glass eyes, and bald-headed chinas, on which wigs could be set, were developed between 1845 and 1860. The top of the head was painted with a black spot like the papier mâché dolls of similar period, although what this denoted is not known. Collectors call them 'black spot' chinas or 'Biedermeiers'. Early chinas usually had sloping shoulders with fine and deep hair moulding; pinkish or reddish cheek tones add still more charm to these dolls. An extremely rare early type consists of a china head on a jointed peg-wooden body with china arms and legs.

## FROZEN CHARLOTTES OR FROZEN CHARLEYS (1850-1914)

These dolls of glazed china throughout are also known as Bathing Dolls. They were usually made with extended, immobile arms with clenched fists and had painted hairstyles. They came in a variety of sizes from miniature to about 50 cm/20 in. Some had short black or blonde brush-stroke hair and others had moulded hair styled as for a little girl. Examples are found with moulded clothes, though these are very rare, and some have moulded boots in varying designs, or moulded bonnets. The china of these Frozen Charlotte-type dolls is either white or pink-toned. As with other chinas, these have been reproduced, the reproductions tending to be flawless. Many of the old dolls seem to have specks of black kiln dust baked into the porcelain and scattered over their bodies, and this can be a clue as to authenticity. Long experience in handling dolls is the best safeguard against reproductions and fakes; the novice collector should take advice.

## FRENCH CHINAS — OR GLAZED FRENCH FASHION DOLLS

Collectors differ in their opinions about categorizing these dolls, some feeling they belong to the chinas with their high glazed porcelain, and others considering that because of their shape, style and method of design they must be regarded as French fashion dolls, their high glaze being

BELOW *Pair of blonde china heads,* left *'Low brow' china 15 cm/6 in high with more common wavy hair low on forehead, good face painting, red line above eyes, 3 sew holes (1890-1900) and* right *china head 12 cm/4¾ in high, with 2 sew holes, child-like face, ears partly showing, often used to depict a boy or man doll (c.1880). (Author's collection).*

incidental. Whichever definition is given to them is up to the individual collector.

The French chinas are rather different in style from the Germans, and have more delicate, understated countenances. Huret, Rohmer, D'Autremont and Barrois, are among the famous names of French doll patentees between 1850-60. These dolls are, in fact, fashion dolls in appearance and are the forerunners of the dolls conventionally called French fashion dolls. Their commercially-made bodies are of many different materials — leather, leather and wood, gutta-percha or tin — and were often marked on the body by the manufacturer. Hurets and Rohmers are particularly sought after by collectors. They differ greatly in design from the German chinas: apart from the more delicate design, they have cutaway heads to enable glass eyes to be inserted, and cork pates over which the wigs were fixed; some had painted eyes. Heads were nailed through the sew holes on to the bodies. Swivel heads were also produced around 1850.

RIGHT Autoperipatetikos *doll with key wind and rare braided hairstyle. She has leather arms and metal feet and wears her original dress. The carton base of the doll reads 'Patented July 15, 1862 also in Europe 20 Dec 1862,' (Chelsea Lion, London).*

## Hairstyles

Many people collect chinas for their different hairstyles, and there is an almost limitless variety, including braided coronets, snoods, centre partings, exposed ears with a bun at the back (like the young Queen Victoria), 'spaniel ears' style flaring at the sides, and the 'painted wagon' style with centre parting and 13 curls around the face ending at the neck. Sometimes the doll's hair line has a straight edge which is a little hard-looking, while others have fine brush strokes framing the face which gives a more delicate look. Some styles are low on the back of the neck and others are painted high on the nape. Obviously it is difficult for the collector to identify unmarked dolls, and it is not even known how or whether they were marked at the time of manufacture. Collectors over the years have given names to different hair styles, such as the snood head china known as the 'Mary Todd Lincoln'. No documentation exists to prove whether this was in fact a portrait of the lady, but her name has been associated with this type of china for many years.

## Ornamentals

The ornamental chinas with exotic features were clearly an attempt by the manufacturer to woo customers. Nothing has been left untried. Trims of every kind were moulded onto the heads — bows, feathers, flowers, bands and snoods, and every kind of hair ornament. Different colours were used for this, gold being greatly favoured. Sometimes a black-haired china would have a gold moulded net over the hair, or a blonde-haired doll would have a black moulded snood. China heads in many different forms and with various hair designs used on Autoperipatetikos bodies (see Mechanical Dolls and Automata, page 46). One particular style of doll with a low snood is known by collectors as 'Empress Eugenie'.

Such wide ranges of chinas exist that one can only assume that they were very popular. Their durability must have made them attractive, for although they were breakable they could be washed by their owners and did not scratch or lose their colour. It must be remembered that toys were not available to children in such abundance.

## LATER CHINAS – 1860 ONWARDS

As the century progressed, the style and form of chinas changed. The most marked difference was in hair colouring: while dark brown and black hair had always been made, suddenly there was a profusion of blondes. It is interesting to speculate why this would have been. Were the manufacturers attempting to increase their range by thinking up innovations, or were they trying to appeal to a completely different market?

Variations of blonde, from honey and strawberry to dark oatmeal, appeared and at the same time there was a discernible difference in the look of the chinas. They became more child-like, with chubby cheeks and short necks; boys and men were depicted with side partings. Was this a subtle attempt at greater child-appeal? The quality of the manufacture, including the fine face painting, remained the same in spite of these changes. Hair styles tended to be short and bobbed and the so-called 'curly top' chinas, with curls all over the head and falling down over the forehead, began to appear. There was the 'Dolly Madison' style with the moulded bow, the so-called 'Highland Mary' with a fringe, the 'Princess Alexandra' with a snood. This doll is the same as the 'Empress Eugenie, and differs only in that the Empress always has pierced ears and the Princess does not. Another style is known as the 'Currier and Ives' with the head band moulded and brought very far forward on the head. Very similar to this is the 'spill curl' in which the head band is further back on the head. Among the well-known German doll makers, who made chinas were Cüno and Otto Dressel, Kestner, Kling and Heubach.

By the 1900s, the age of the china had passed, to be replaced by other kinds of dolls. The quality had been lost, definition was poor, and it would be left to the doll collector to rekindle interest in these once popular dolls.

Even among collectors in Europe, the popularity of chinas waned a few years ago because of a spate of reproductions, while in the US they were less favoured than fine quality bisque dolls. This kept the price of chinas unrealistically low. Although their popularity and price have now increased, they are still attractive to the collector.

## WHERE TO BEGIN – CHINAS

**LIMITED BUDGET DOLLS** The later chinas are lower in price than the earlier ones and small chinas with simple hairstyles can be picked up quite inexpensively.

**MIDDLE PRICE RANGE AND TOP QUALITY CHINAS** The earlier dolls command a higher price and the chinas with elaborate hairstyles and glass eyes are at the top of the range.

# PARIAN DOLLS

Most dolls heads are made from a fine, matt porcelain called bisque. Parian is a form of bisque porcelain.

The United Federation of Doll Clubs (UFDC) in the USA defines Parian as unglazed porcelain (fine white bisque), without tinting. The word parian comes from Paros in Greece where white marble was found. 'Parian ware' was the term given to entirely white, marble-like items, such as figures, and the substance was soon adopted by porcelain manufacturers for use in doll making: the so-called 'Parian' dolls were made between 1850-80.

RIGHT *Rare Parian shoulder head doll, the so-called 'Princess Augusta Victoria' with beautifully moulded elaborate hair, pierced ears and moulded ruffled collar with modelled cross (1870). (Author's collection).*

The Parians are always assumed to be German and are thought to have been made in the Dresden potteries as well as in other parts of Germany. They usually have golden hair. Documentary evidence in the form of manuals or catalogues relating to dolls being made at Dresden, has never been found. Were dolls not considered worthy of note and therefore not included in sales catalogues? It is hard to believe that this was the case since the quality of design, modelling and workmanship are so obviously high. A little information has recently come to light, which confirms the origins of these 'Dresden' heads.

RIGHT *'Countess Dagmar' Parian shoulder head doll, 42.5 cm/17 in with fine hair modelling, blue painted eyes with red eye dots and red upper line. She has a moulded blouse, stuffed fabric body, bisque arms and lower legs with black painted boots, red laces and blue painted garters. (Author's collection).*

Some Parian manufacturers put makers' marks on their wares. C.F. Kling & Co. 1836-1925 of Ohrdruf, Thuringia, Germany who made jointed all-porcelain dolls, marked some of their blonde shoulder heads with a 'K' inside a bell. Among the numbers found with the bell symbol are '148 0', '186.5', '189 3' and '123 2', and so on. Simon & Halbig 1870-1925 of Gräfenhain in Thuringia, Germany also made Parian dolls' heads with moulded blonde hair and fine quality painting. These are usually marked S*H with the numerical size in the middle. Dernheim, Koch & Fischer (1860-1900) Gräfenroda, Thuringia marked their wares DKF. They made Parian heads, notably one of fine quality with the 'Dresden' flower decoration, each petal standing out separately. George Borgfeldt & Co. 1881-1925 of Berlin and New York made and imported dolls and donated a fine collection of Parian dolls to the Museum of the City of New York. Some of the marks included on their heads are '5E', '2K3', '5M5', 'G', and '505'.

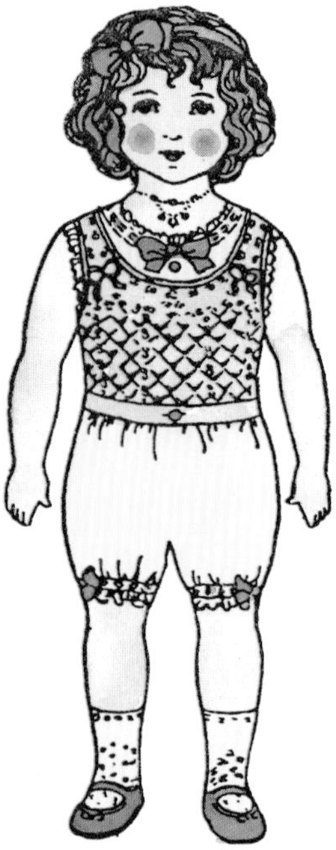

When Parian dolls are marked the mark will probably be inside or on the back of the shoulder plate. Like china heads, Parian heads are found without bodies and were probably sold in a similar way for home-made bodies to be attached to them. Interestingly, some china and Parian dolls appear to have been made from the same moulds but the Parians tend to look more realistic than the chinas with their high glaze, because skin tones and textures are more finely portrayed in this medium.

The face painting on Parian dolls is generally of excellent quality and definition and the eyes, which are generally painted, are usually blue. Brown-eyed and bisque Parians are considered rarer and were evidently less popular in their day. Glass-eyed dolls are also found on rare occasions. Generally speaking, with the exception of the extremely early dolls, rare examples often denote a less popular time, with fewer of the type originally being made. Obviously dolls which were popular were made in greater numbers and these are the ones which we find in quantity today. Oddly enough, the dolls which were less popular yesterday and which are now hard to find have become

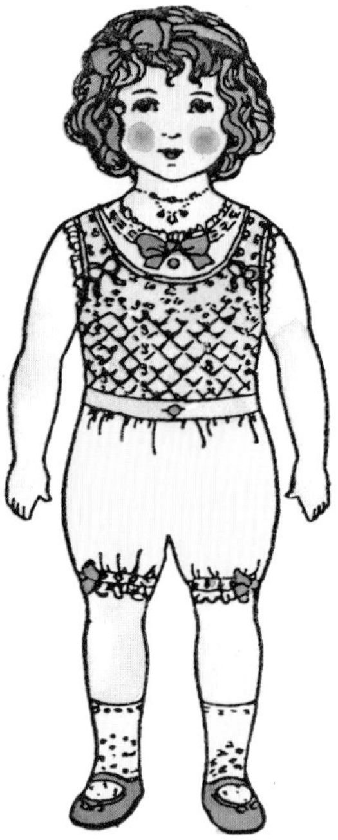

UNITED
FEDERATION
OF
DOLL CLUBS
10th Annual
Exhibition
Kansas City
1959
PORTMAN
INTERNATIONAL
ANTIQUE

the more treasured and expensive collectors' items.

## BODIES

Parian heads are found on as complete a range of bodies as are chinas. Sometimes they are on the home-made creations of the household nursery, while the commercially-made bodies are of cloth and generally have Parian limbs. More rarely, they also have cloth legs and leather arms.

## PARIAN HEADS AND THEIR IDENTIFICATION

As with chinas, collectors needed to devise a way of identifying the usually unmarked Parian dolls, so they gave them names, some of which are shared with chinas, for example, 'Dolly Madison' (1870-80), 'Countess Dagmar' with both blonde and black hair (1870), 'Empress Eugenie', 'Princess Alexandra', 'Alice in Wonderland', 'Jenny Lind' (1870), 'Highland Mary', 'Mary Todd Lincoln' and 'Adelina Patti', to name the best known.

However, certain heads are found only on Parians, as if they were produced either by a different manufacturer, or their design lent itself more readily to Parian. Generally speaking, there are far more elaborately decorated Parian dolls in existence than china. Parian versions of 'Empress Eugenie' are sometimes referred to as 'Lucy'. This wonderful head with its silver-white feather and purple lustre tassel has an exquisitely moulded, firmly structured face.

Glass eyes are also to be found on Parian dolls and are the most highly sought after of the type, commanding high prices. Some of the most prized Parians have elaborately-moulded frills on their shoulder plates and exquisite hair ornamentation. Another doll not found in china is the so-called 'blue scarf' doll. This is said to represent the Empress Louise of Prussia at Schönbrunn Palace. These dolls were reproduced by Emma Clear of the USA between 1940 and 1950 and are marked with her name and the year.

'Miss Liberty' is a seldom seen example; she has a lustre crown and streamers, blonde or brown hair, painted or glass eyes, and moulded ear-rings or pierced ears. 'Princess Augusta Victoria' (1870) is another Parian not found in china. She has a moulded hair band, high curls, moulded, ruffled collar and modelled cross. The so called 'flat top' is an interesting doll, found both in Parian and in china. Dating from between 1840-50, she has a flat top to her head and rows of little sausage curls coming down around it — a most unrealistic hairstyle, more than a little reminiscent of a Frankenstein monster! 'Flat tops' are found with either painted or glass eyes. 'Amelia Bloomer' is a most interesting and seldom seen Parian, with painted eyes and short, cropped hair. It is not known if this Parian was actually meant to be a portrait of the famous lady from American history herself, or just a similar type. Amelia Bloomer (1818-1894) was a pioneer of women's rights in the USA, which may be why the doll is portrayed with short cropped hair.

There are also a number of stone bisque dolls with a wide assortment of hats, bonnets and bows which are unique to the Parian type; one in particular has a moulded fur hat and collar. Stone bisque is a coarse white bisque of poorer quality than most Parians because it is made from less finely ground clay. Interesting features are often found on these dolls, however, and this is their attraction — not the quality of their manufacture.

## COLLECTING PARIANS – WHERE TO START

◆ **LIMITED BUDGET** Dolls with simple hairstyles, painted eyes and less facial definition should be priced accordingly. The stone bisques may sometimes be in this class because of their relative lack of quality, but they often pick up points for their innovative design.

◆ **MEDIUM AND TOP PRICE RANGE DOLLS** Glass-eyed Parians are in this range. Generally, the more elaborate the modelling, the better the quality. The inclusion of costume (or not) will affect the cost.

LEFT *Rare Parian shoulder head doll 32.5 cm/13 in tall with painted eyes and moulded blonde hair. The head is turned to one side. She is the chubby-cheeked variety of child-like Parian with Parian arms, stuffed body and Parian limbs with moulded purple lustre decorated bootees. She is in her original box with a note fastened to the dress which reads 'given to a baby October 9 1864, the day she was born'. A note on the red, white and blue award reads 'ribbon won during the Civil War'. She also has a ribbon which reads '2nd Prize, United Federation of Doll Clubs 10th Annual Exhibition, Kansas City 1959' and another which reads 'Portman International Antique Dolls, Toys, & Miniatures Fair - Second'. (Author's collection).*

# WAX DOLLS

From medieval times, wax was established in Europe as an artistic medium; funeral effigies and floral displays were often made in wax. By the 18th century, it was an established doll material throughout Europe and in the USA.

Wax dolls are certainly among the most beautiful dolls available to the collector. (See English Wax Dolls page 74). Wax as a medium gives rich, authentically natural skin tones with a translucent quality which cannot be achieved in bisque.

As a soft medium, of course, wax was subject to damage and destruction and many examples have not survived. Prior to the early 19th century, the dolls were sometimes eaten by mice, until the manufacturers put something into the wax to make it less desirable to rodents. Some wax dolls melted when left by the fire and others simply got sat upon.

Contrary to popular belief, wax dolls will not melt simply in a warm room, but if left in a sunny window the colour pigments will fade and the wax may become quite white, while the limbs, covered up with clothes, are likely to retain their original colour.

## WAX DOLL MANUFACTURE

In the 18th and 19th centuries, the better-class dolls had solid wax heads, wax limbs and stuffed fabric bodies.

To make a wax head, a sculpture would be made from which a mould would be taken. This was warmed and the liquid wax was then poured in — sometimes in two or three stages to get the right thickness. White lead and carmine would sometimes be added for colour and, when set, the mould would be taken off and the finishing touches put to the doll. Eye holes would be cut for insertion of the glass eyes, eyelashes would be added and the hair fixed in clumps into the wax of the head. The head would then be dusted with potato starch, a powdered alabaster or pumice to give a good complexion. After this, the cheeks were tinted with rouge and the lips and nostrils touched with vermillion. Holes were made in the breastplate of the doll's head so that it could be sewn onto the cloth body. In the same way, the limbs were fashioned and sewn on.

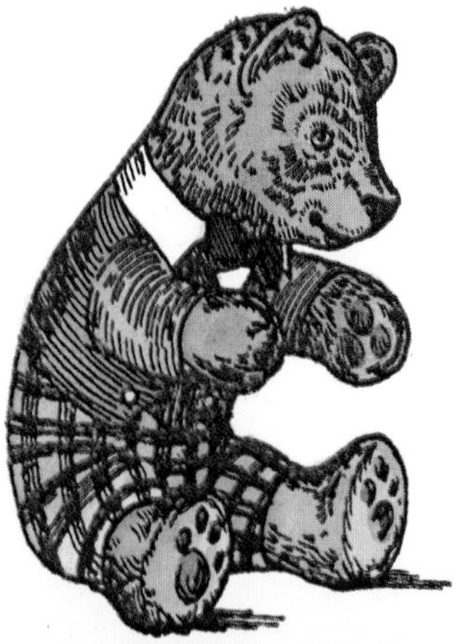

RIGHT *Pierotti-type, English poured wax doll, 60 cm/24 in high with glass eyes. The trunk is stuffed with horsehair and the limbs are poured wax. The dress and matching hat are of paper taffeta and lace. (Author's collection).*

ABOVE *Wax-over-papier-mâché shoulder plate 'slit head' doll. She is 47.5 cm/19 in tall (Author's collection).*

RIGHT *Wax-over-papier-mâché shoulder head doll with fixed blue eyes. The wig is mohair and the limbs are also wax-over-papier-mâché. She stands 72.5 cm/29 in high and wears her original clothing. Probably French, C. 1870.*

## DIPPED WAX DOLLS

Wax is an expensive material and when mass production started in the mid-19th century, ways had to be found to cheapen manufacture, for example by using a papier mâché core and wax-dipping it and thus limiting the amount of wax needed.

Papier mâché core dolls' heads would sometimes be glued to the body. The wax on the poured wax dolls varies in colour from a very hot pink, through the various flesh tones to pale pink. Only the early, almost pure beeswax dolls have a telltale yellowish complexion. Unfortunately, over the years the dolls with a heavy dusting of pumice may have turned a dirty-looking grey colour, as the layer of pumice solidified and then discoloured. This can prove difficult to remove and should be left to the experts.

## SLIT-HEAD DOLLS

Of the very early dipped wax dolls we know very little, and probably never will discover much, but their charm and their inevitable ringlets link their past to our present. These early dolls, made from wax over papier mâché, often have just a slit in the top of the head — hence the nick-name 'slit head' — through which the hair is distributed and then glued down and formed into ringlets. Some are also found with a hole cut at the back of the head with a papier mâché pate fixed over it, evidently to enable the eyes to be secured. This is usually waxed over and the wig glued over that. The glass eyes in wax dolls made before 1850 were without pupils and were very dark, almost black in colour. Some examples have moving eyes which were opened and shut by means of a wire coming out of the body at the waistline. These were probably introduced around 1825. Eyebrow details were usually painted onto the papier mâché before dipping. Wax dolls are often found with extremely crazed faces. The seasonal expansion and contraction of the papier mâché layer beneath the wax would have caused the wax to crack all over the surface. Ideally as even a temperature as is possible with today's central heating, is most suitable for these dolls, but for many it is too late. They lose their charm and appeal if restored and waxed over, and should be left alone.

The bodies, legs and feet of these slit-head dolls are crudely stuffed, the feet usually turning inwards giving a pigeon-toed effect; the arms are usually of leather. Curiously, the dolls with brown leather arms usually have only three fingers on each hand; while those with white kid arms have the usual five. On most examples, the ringlets are still intact, leaving one to marvel at the workmanship which could produce this effect lasting well over a century. The most striking feature of all is the amazing smile on these dolls' faces; almost every example smiles as if she has been keeping an amusing secret for over 100 years.

## POURED WAX DOLLS

The majority of the best pure wax dolls were made in England and many examples by the most well known names, among them Pierotti, Montanari, Marsh, Meech and Peck are with us today. Most of the 'poured wax' dolls, which is the name given to wax dolls without papier mâché cores, are unmarked and most collectors will refer to a Pierotti 'type' doll or a Montanari 'type' doll as they cannot be identified with any degree of certainty. In extremely rare cases, a Montanari doll may be found bearing a signature in brownish ink on the lower left hand corner of the torso.

Rare also are the marked Pierotti dolls, with the name scratched roughly on to the back of the doll's head. Often the only identification on a doll is the Hamley's toy shop stamp sometimes to be found on the front of the body, but this will not reveal the identity of the manufacturer.

LEFT *Rare poured-wax 1920s lady doll, 60 cm/24 in tall. Her poured wax limbs have rigid arms and moveable legs. Her shoes are moulded. (Author's collection).*

Wax dolls were also made in France, and in the mid-19th century Sonneberg in Germany was famous for them. These heads were usually reinforced with plaster. Fritz Bartenstein (1880-98) of Hüttensteinach, Germany was a well known maker of wax dolls. He is particularly famous for his double-faced doll, one laughing and one crying. The head could be turned by the movement of a string, and one of the faces would be hidden by a hood. There is a similar type of doll shown on page 94. He also made his two-faced doll in wax-over-papier-mâché with the face moving horizontally under a metal cap. The body is of cardboard, and sometimes bears the Bartenstein stamp in purple ink. Other early wax-over-papier-mâché dolls include the so-called 'pumpkin head' dolls with fancy moulded hairstyles, stuffed bodies, wooden limbs and either painted feet or painted red or green boots; they have black pupilless eyes.

BELOW *English poured wax doll, 42.5 cm/17 in tall with poured wax limbs. She is a late Pierotti-type doll with hair, eyelashes and eyebrows inserted into the wax. She has a stuffed body stamped with the Hamleys Toy Shop stamp of the period and is in mint condition. She is dressed in her original white cotton dress, underwear and straw bonnet. (Author's collection).*

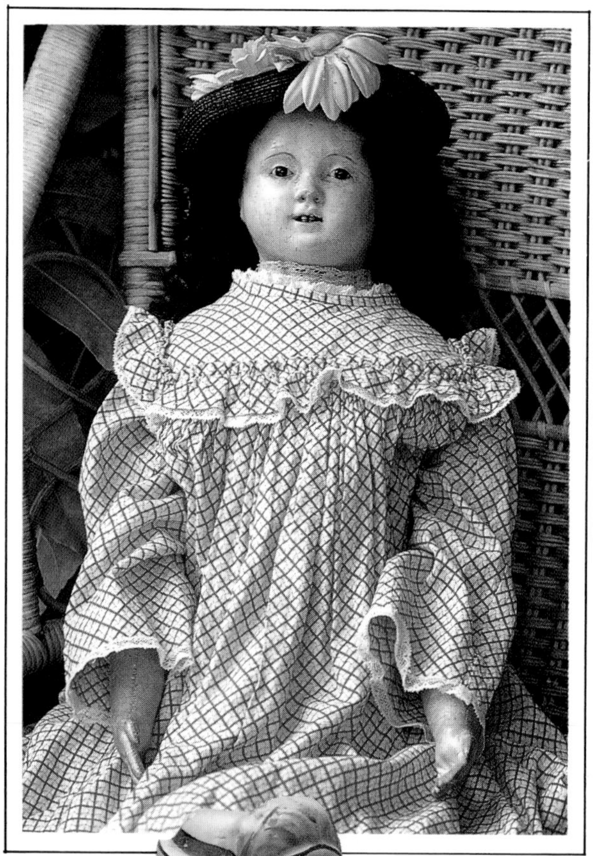

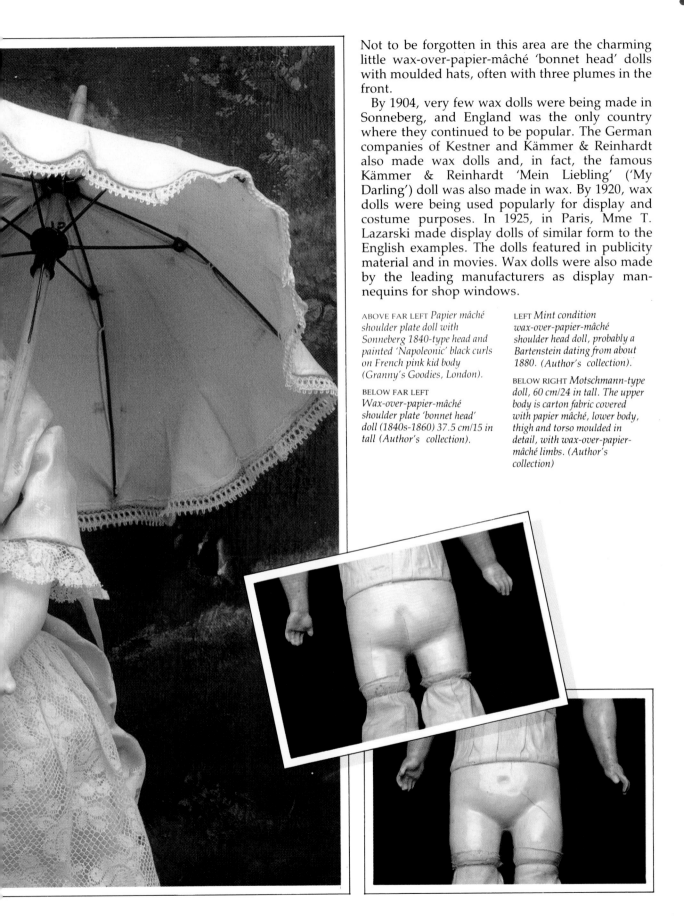

Not to be forgotten in this area are the charming little wax-over-papier-mâché 'bonnet head' dolls with moulded hats, often with three plumes in the front.

By 1904, very few wax dolls were being made in Sonneberg, and England was the only country where they continued to be popular. The German companies of Kestner and Kämmer & Reinhardt also made wax dolls and, in fact, the famous Kämmer & Reinhardt 'Mein Liebling' ('My Darling') doll was also made in wax. By 1920, wax dolls were being used popularly for display and costume purposes. In 1925, in Paris, Mme T. Lazarski made display dolls of similar form to the English examples. The dolls featured in publicity material and in movies. Wax dolls were also made by the leading manufacturers as display mannequins for shop windows.

ABOVE FAR LEFT *Papier mâché shoulder plate doll with Sonneberg 1840-type head and painted 'Napoleonic' black curls on French pink kid body (Granny's Goodies, London).*

BELOW FAR LEFT *Wax-over-papier-mâché shoulder plate 'bonnet head' doll (1840s-1860) 37.5 cm/15 in tall (Author's collection).*

LEFT *Mint condition wax-over-papier-mâché shoulder head doll, probably a Bartenstein dating from about 1880. (Author's collection).*

BELOW RIGHT *Motschmann-type doll, 60 cm/24 in tall. The upper body is carton fabric covered with papier mâché, lower body, thigh and torso moulded in detail, with wax-over-papier-mâché limbs. (Author's collection)*

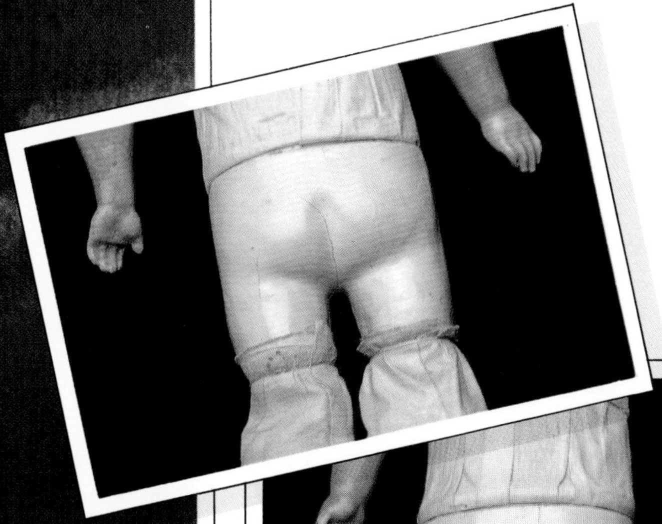

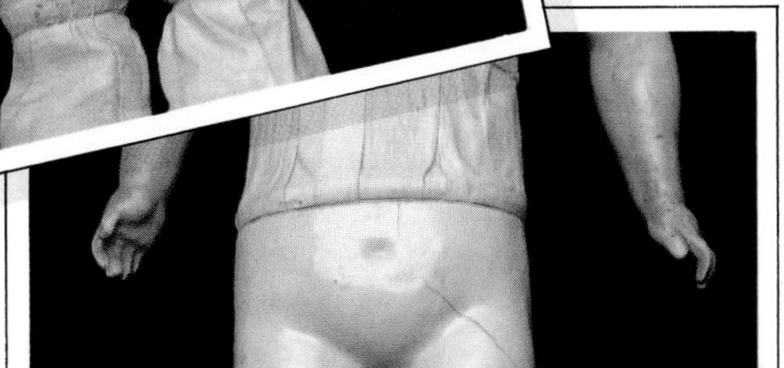

## COLLECTING WAX DOLLS - WHERE TO START

**LIMITED BUDGET DOLLS** Early slit-head type dolls have not increased in value commercially over the past five years or so, and they make a very interesting and worthwhile area for the novice collector on a limited budget. Many fine examples can be found, each one unique, and undoubtedly they will increase greatly in value when one of the major doll-buying countries, like Japan, finally discovers them. Poor or damaged examples can be found at very low prices.

**MIDDLE-OF-THE-RANGE-DOLLS** Fine examples of slit-head dolls with good costumes and in excellent condition can be found in the middle price range; this is true also of pumpkin-head, two-faced and bonnet-head dolls.

**TOP-OF-THE-RANGE-DOLLS** Poured wax dolls appear to fluctuate in price from year to year, but a perfect example with original clothes will obviously always fetch a higher price than one with cracks and no clothes. The best poured wax dolls are in the upper price range of the wax field. If well done, restoration on a poured wax doll is not quite so seriously regarded in terms of price as it would be on a bisque doll. As with most dolls price is greatly affected by condition of clothing, and fine early clothes on a poured wax doll will enhance its value.

# PAPIER MACHE DOLLS

Papier mâché — literally 'chewed' paper — is apparently a term with English origins and not, as most people would imagine, French. There were many methods and formulas for its composition, but all were based on raw paper pulp moistened with water. To this a filler was added, such as flour, meal, sand, clay, whiting or chalk, and a binder was used to hold the substances together; this was usually glue or a gelatinous material like starch paste or gum arabic.

Some papier mâché doll manufacturers would add resins, oils and repellants to make the dolls less desirable to rodents, and some would add deodorisers to minimise the odours of the glue. Each manufacturer would strive to keep his particular formula secret.

Papier mâché can be made of any vegetable or animal fibre. Unless it is possible to analyze a head, it is almost impossible to know exactly which additives were used, but the German industry generally employed watered-down animal glue.

## ORIGINS OF PAPIER MÂCHÉ? DOLLS

When one considers the papier mâché doll and the nature of the market is served, it is obvious that it could not be expensively made. The factories making these dolls needed to be near paper mills to have easy access to their raw materials, and this led to the establishment of certain areas of manufacture. Papier mâché dolls came primarily from England, Germany and the USA and, to a lesser extent, from France. Nuremburg, in South Germany, had a paper mill in the 14th century, as did Sonneberg somewhat later. Rye flour used in the process came from the valleys beneath the wooded mountains and this region with its easy access to both paper pulp and flour would have been naturally suitable for the development of the papier mâché doll industry.

Paper pulp had obvious advantages over clay: it was lighter, did not break as easily, dried in the open air instead of a furnace, and took a wider variety of finishes. Japanning — a hard laquer — was one embellishment of papier mâché, while wax was the favoured finish in the English doll-making industry. The heads were often made and sold on their own so that homemade cloth bodies could be attached to them. Often these were

LEFT *Wax-over-papier-mâché bride, 57.7 cm/23 in tall in mint condition. She has a straw-filled body with very short composition arms and composition legs. Her mohair wig is glued to a carton pate and her glass eyes are fixed. Her bridal gown, underwear, shoes and socks are all original. The dress is of oyster paper taffeta with lace trims. There are tiny wax flowers in her hair and bouquet. (Author's collection).*

ABOVE *1880s German papier mâché doll in original clothing. Her cotton bonnet has silk and malibu trim, and she is also wearing three underskirts, a cotton dress and a cotton cape with lace and silk trimming, and a bib with* baby *embroidered on it. Queen Victoria presented this doll to the daughter of one of her ladies-in-waiting, in 1898. A letter recounting the incident still accompanies the doll, together with a picture of the doll and the child. (Leona Gerwat-Clark collection).*

simply stuffed cloth, and the variety of standards in these homemade bodies gives rise to a certain inconsistency. Sometimes the arms are of leather and sometimes of cloth; many are crudely stump-shaped. The heads were simply glued on to the body at the shoulderplate.

Papier mâché is a substance that can be produced quite easily in a small workshop, or even at home. Some interesting examples exist of papier mâché dolls made by gifted home dollmakers.

## MAKING THE DOLL'S HEADS – METHODS OF MANUFACTURE

The dolls' heads would first be modelled by our early 'doll artists', who have left us a wonderful record of historic hair fashions with elaborate coiffures, ringlets and braids. Unfortunately these artists are usually undocumented and their creations reach out to us from faceless progenitors.

'The mould makers, who probably worked in their own homes, would make the moulds from the modelled forms. The moulds were often made in several parts and the lines on some heads will sometimes indicate how many they were made from. The papier mâché-mixture would then be pressed into the mould and allowed to dry. One-piece moulds would sometimes be used, especially for small heads. They were usually made of plaster of Paris or gypsum, and various places on the head would have to be reinforced, the seams, the nose, and so on. Linen or muslin was used as a reinforcing material, and after the head was completed it had to be dressed for painting. Filler and an undercoat would be used to dress the heads in this way, and chalk, clay, gesso, gypsum or plaster, in various thicknesses, was most common.

The skills of the finishers were all-important as it was upon the effects they produced that the whole doll would ultimately be judged (with the exception of the clothing). The finisher gave the doll its skin pigments, eyes, eyebrow definitions, lip and hair colouring, as well as any extra decoration which might be included. Finally, a protective coat of glue wash or varnish would be applied. The glue wash was somewhat unsuccessful as we see now with the French pink kid-bodied papier mâché dolls, in which the shine almost always appears to have been washed off the doll.

## TYPES OF PAPIER MÂCHÉ DOLLS

There is much documentary evidence on the manufacture of papier mâché dolls' heads in the early 19th century by factories in the Sonneberg and Nuremburg districts of south Germany, and the majority of heads will have come from these areas.

## GEORGIAN WAX-OVER PAPIER MÂCHÉ DOLLS

In the first quarter of the 19th century 'Georgian wax-overs', as they are sometimes referred to, were being produced in England. These are generally regarded as wax rather than papier mâché dolls, but they had papier mâché cores. The faces were flat and smiling faces, and the heads are often not quite smooth, perhaps through warping

ABOVE *Wax-over-papier-mâché shoulder plate doll, dating from the first half of the 19th century. She has a horsehair-stuffed body and arms of maroon leather with four fingers and a thumb and stuffed pigeon-toed feet. Her mohair ringlets are glued to her head and her long pantaloons and cotton dress with blue silk trims and lace and silk hat are original. The crazing on the face is commonly found on these dolls. (Author's collection).*

RIGHT *Papier mâché shoulder head doll with bent composition arms and legs and horsehair-stuffed cloth body. The doll has a note stitched under her dress from the original owner, who was given the doll which was called 'Rose Ann'. (Collection of Naomi Gerwat-Clark).*

as a result of not being carefully pressed or dried. It is difficult to give any other explanation for their crude form. In spite of this, their serene charm is unique. Hairstyles on the moulded-hair dolls often help to date them. The portrait-type dolls depicted famous personalities of the period, whose hairstyles may be familiar to us today from contemporary paintings.

## Greiner And Pre-Greiner Dolls

Ludwig Greiner was a German dollmaker who emigrated to the USA and opened a factory in Philadelphia. He was issued with the first US patent for a doll's head in the US, patent No. 10770, dated March 30, 1858. Sometimes his heads bear a paper label with the patent date on it. However, it is known that Greiner was producing dolls in Philadelphia as early as 1840. In fact, a Greiner doll has been found with a newspaper dated 1845 stuffed inside the head and obviously put there during manufacture.

The Greiner finishing glaze was very durable and his dolls have come down to us in good condition. Greiner only made heads; the bodies were generally homemade, from crudely-stuffed cloth, sometimes with leather arms. Commercially-produced bodies could also be purchased, and these were available from Jacob Lacmann, also of Philadelphia, who was in business between 1860 and 1883. Lacmann's bodies were made of cloth with leather arms and hands. The dolls had red- or blue-striped socks and sewn leather boots in red, blue or yellow.

Greiner dolls are seldom, if ever, found outside the USA and clearly were not exported.

A similar type of doll is known as the pre-Greiner. These dolls obviously come into the same category as the Greiner dolls but predate the patent. The finish is finer and the glaze thinner, and the dolls have either blown glass or painted eyes. The earliest examples have moulded hair braided on each side at the front and wound under the ears to join a braided coil at the back of the head. These dolls date from about 1837-1840 and are clearly intended to represent Queen Victoria, who is often shown wearing this hair style at the period.

It is often speculated that the socalled pre-Greiner dolls with glass eyes were imported heads and were never made by Greiner in the US, but it is also postulated that when Greiner emigrated to the United States, as an experienced dollmaker, he would have taken with him quantities of blown glass eyes. When his stock was used up, he would have had difficulty replacing them in Philadelphia and would perhaps have switched, at least temporarily, to painted eyes. He must have found a way to make the glass eyes in the United States,

FIRST PLACE
LEHIGH VALLEY DOLL STUDY CLUB
REGIONAL
INTERNATIONAL ANTIQUE
FIRST
DOLLS, TOYS & MINIATURES FAIR

and began producing glass-eyed dolls even before he took out his patent.

Personally, I doubt very much that the early, so-called pre-Greiner heads were imported into the United States. This would have added greatly to the cost of the finished product and made it over-priced. I believe that the so-called 'pre-Greiner' dolls were, in fact, Greiner's own early dolls.

Greiner's patent was extended to 1872, as is demonstrated by paper labels found in later heads. Greiner and pre-Greiner are terms which often confuse the novice collector, but can be useful, when clearly defined, in the search for knowledge.

## M & S Superior Dolls

This name has been found on paper labels on composition heads produced during the 1880s and 1890s. The initials are believed to refer to the firm of Müller and Strassberger of Sonneberg. The dolls are similar in style to the Greiner dolls, with moulded hair, and tend to be blonde. The high glaze on these dolls, which was meant to be a 'superior' finish was, in fact, thick and brittle and subject to scratching. These dolls have not survived as well as the Greiners and their faces always seem to be damaged. Furthermore, the glaze has yellowed with age, becoming less realistic and less attractive than the finish on the Greiner dolls. These dolls are seldom found outside the USA.

## Milliners' Models And High Coiffure Dolls

This is the name given by some collectors to papier mâché heads with kid bodies, and non-articulated wooden limbs. However, there is no evidence to suggest that they were milliners' dolls and the elaborate coiffures on many of them would have precluded the donning of a sample hat anyway. In addition, the bodies are rigid, making the pulling on and off of clothes extremely difficult, if not impossible. It is even doubtful whether these dolls were used to exhibit samples of the latest fashions as has been suggested. However, when describing unmarked dolls whose manufacturer is unknown the collector needs a means of identifying them to others and very many of the type names given to dolls have arisen, sometimes long ago, in response to this need. The little milliners' models as we shall therefore call them, range in size from about 15 cm/16 in to 50 cm/20 in and the high styles of coiffures date from between 1810 and 1820.

As the century progressed, innovations were created, and one of these was the swivel neck doll. It was not altogether successful in papier mâché because the material could not withstand the inevitable wear on the socket. By the last quarter of the century, many famous doll-making names were on the scene: Mlle Rohmer, the famous French doll maker, Fleischmann, Heubach, Fleischmann & Bloedel, Handwerke, Kämmer & Reinhardt, Kestner, Schilling, Simon & Halbig and many others. Most of them had their origins in pre-1900 papier mâché heads. Few of these later dolls were of the moulded hair variety: most would have had wigs and resembled the bisque dolls in style. Many of the famous doll-making families of Germany intermarried, and an active exchange of ideas obviously went on.

## Collecting Papier Mâché Dolls — Where To Start

**LIMITED BUDGET DOLLS** Cheap examples of these dolls are rarely to be found but dolls in poor condition may be inexpensive on occasion.

**MIDDLE RANGE DOLLS AND HIGHER-PRICED DOLLS** The Georgian wax-over-papier-mâchés and the Greiners and Superiors are similarly priced, although the larger glass-eyed Greiners may fetch high prices, as do the early milliners' models with high coiffures.

LEFT *Papier mâché shoulder plate Greiner doll, 60 cm/24 in tall with stuffed body, painted sad eyes, painted moulded black hair, leather arms and stuffed legs. Tucked into her dress was a note which read 'This doll belonged to Sarah Neemes, born in England June 16, 1828 and was probably brought with her when she came to America in 1836'. It is also likely that this doll was made in America. (Author's collection).*

# MECHANICAL DOLLS & AUTOMATA

The uses of hydraulic and pneumatic processes for movement were replaced when the Renaissance brought with it the mechanical skills of the clockwork movement. Metal pins moving against a cylinder could be used to create sound. The way was at last clear for musical toys, and eventually shops flourished with such rich names as "Edlins Rational Repository of Amusement and Instruction" in Bond Street, London around 1811.

Each new technological era brings with it man's latest attempts at making even more perfect images of himself. In the 18th century, the production of automata reached its zenith. The musical automata were not so much working figures as musical instruments inside an exquisite human shape. An example is 'The Dulcimer Player', made in 1780 by the Germans Roentgen and Kintzing for Queen Marie-Antoinette. Music was composed especially for it by Glück. The equally well-known 'Juvenile Artist' by Jaquet-Droz, produced in 1774, is another fine example of a lifelike form. He is a handsome young boy who sits at a table, holding a pen. So sophisticated was the mechanism that the doll could write long sentences. Later well-known makers of automata of the period were Maillardet, Johannes Jean Maelzel (b. 1783) and Baron von Kempelen. Von Kempelen's machines could even utter the different vowel sounds. Maelzel won an award in the Exhibition of French Industry of 1823 for a talking doll comprising a bellows action activated by arm movements sending air from a read to a voice box. The resulting 'Pa pa' could then be modified to repeat the 'Ma ma' sound. Most of the good 19th century automata have Swiss movements and French bodies.

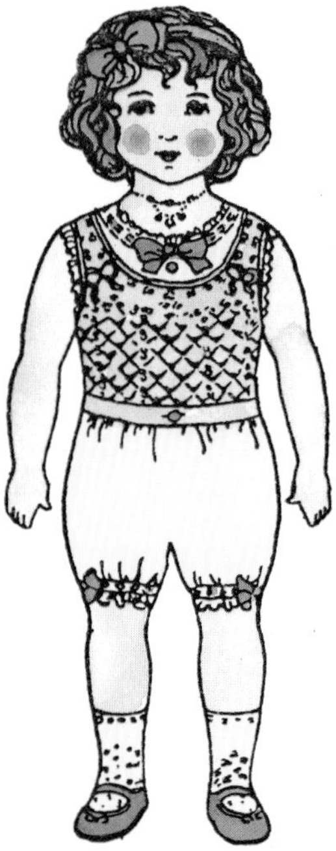

Very often the automata are attributed to an earlier date than they should be, due to misdating of the clothing as much as to a general lack of information on the subject. Reference to the early catalogues with very clear pictorial descriptions gives us the dating clues. As late as 1911 Gaston Decamps (who died in 1972 aged 90), the son of Ernest Decamps, produced a catalogue containing a great variety of performing animals, foxes, elephants, birds, cats, mice, dogs, and so on. A series of simpler 'pull along' toys was also included and in these a doll was mounted on a platform with wheels, the movement of which would activate some part of the doll.

*Fiddler automation with bisque Jumeau head, made for M.M. Heriot et Cie, of Paris in the 1880s. The jacket is original (Edinburgh Museum of Childhood).*

BELOW *A Leopold Lambert musical automaton, all original, French c. 1880. The closed-mouth, bisque head is stamped in red 'Déposé tête Jumeau Bte. S.G.D./G. 1'. The eyes are fixed and the ears pierced. The forearms are bisque. The head and arms move to the musical movement activated by a stop/start mechanism in the base. The doll is 41.25 cm/16½ in tall. (Chelsea Lion, London).*

## TALKING DOLLS

Johannes Mäelzel was granted a patent for his talking doll in 1824. Various methods were used to achieve the sound of the human voice. The bellows produced the initial sound, but a 19th century innovation was the addition of a reed which would produce sound from the air blown over it by the bellows. The bellows could be activated by pulling strings, moving a limb or making some other movement of the doll's body.

Alexandre Nicholas Théroude was a well-known mid-19th century mechanical toy maker, working from 5 Rue Montmorency, Paris. His 1852 patent describes his talking doll process by which the doll said 'Ma ma', 'Pa pa' and 'Cou cou'. There is some evidence of a talented talking-dollmaker working in London in the 1850s, but sadly his name has not survived. In the 1880s Charles Motschmann, a well-known dollmaker, also produced a type of talking doll which could produce sound when the head was pushed down. By 1855 the clockmaker Jules Nicholas Steiner was on the Paris scene. To his 'Ma ma' and 'Pa pa' voice box, he added, in 1890, a moving head, arms and legs. His virtually indestructable mechanism in the torso of the doll has insured that most examples of this doll are still found in working order today. His patent name for this doll was, Bébé Premier Pas (First Step Baby). The Premier Pas head, which does not bear a maker's mark, had an open mouth with two rows of sharp, pointed teeth. Some people find this is a rather sinister and unattractive aspect of the doll, though the more purist collector would see it as an unusual and therefore appealing attribute.

Dolls of this period were to continue to have limited speech functions, but by the 1880s it was also possible to introduce recorded speech. Thomas Alva Edison's talking doll patent of 1878 produced a crude steel torso, concealing a phonogram. A Simon & Halbig head was attached. Production was several hundred dolls a day, but few have survived. In 1877, Edison had invented the first crude talking machine; with this, dolls' tongues were unleashed and they began to sing all manner of songs and nursery thymes. A miniature version of a phonograph was inserted into the doll's body and different songs could be played merely by changing the wax cylinders.

The most frequently found phonograph doll, if frequent is the word, as they are still very rare, is the Jumeau Bébé Phonographe of 1893-1898. Numerous other companies imitated Jumeau. A phonograph doll must indeed have been a treasured item for a child. From this period onward, every possible method was used to produce realistic speech. The doll always cried 'Ma ma' and 'Pa pa' when the leg was moved, or its foot was pushed or a lever moved in the back of its head.

LEFT *A 'kicking Steiner' doll (French, 1875–80), also known as Bébé Premier Pas. Her cardboard body contains a key wind mechanism activating her legs – hence the nickname. She also has a voice-box and says 'Mama' and 'Papa'. (Author's collection.)*

BELOW *A fine example of 'The Smoker' automaton, 50 cm/20 in high. There is a key wind mechanism to turn the head, smoke the pipe and tap the cane. The movement is by Leopold Lambert. (Author's collection.)*

## WALKING DOLLS AND THE SWIMMING DOLL

The quest for sound also led to the quest for life-like movement, and numerous innovators endeavoured to achieve this in a multitude of ways. Steiner's *Premier Pas* doll, of course, belongs under both headings with its leg movement, but the prize for a purely walking doll must go to the Autoperipatetikos (Greek for 'walking-about-by-itself') doll. These dolls also appear to have virtually indestructable movements and are operated on a key winding mechanism. Invented by Enoch Rice Morrison and patented on 15 July 1862, the bodies are found with numerous different types of heads ranging from Parian, wax, papier mâché and china. They had little metal feet which walked with great style beneath their crinoline skirts. This is the most commonly found type and while there are rarer examples such as a Napoleon III doll, the male forms are perhaps less appealing than the crinoline lady dolls. The prize should probably be shared between Morrison and William F. Goodwin of New York who, in 1868, patented a very realistic doll pushing a pram. In Paris in 1876, M. Martin produced the swimming doll, later called 'Ondine' with a Simon & Halbig head. Her body was of cork which made her float. She could swim on her back as well as her front and did a perfect breast stroke. Out of the water, the strange angle of her legs and arms gave her an almost frog-like look.

FRAGILE
FRAGILE

LEFT TO RIGHT *Bisque-headed magician possibly by Decamps 85 cm/34 in tall; jester with a blackamoor trying to escape from a crate by Decamps; hunch-backed Pierrot and his monkey with eleven different movements by Vichy. The dunce, also by Vichy has had the clockwork mechanism replaced by an electrical one; the same modification has been made to the seated black lyre-player which bears the Vichy maker's plaque. (Sotheby's New York.)*

ABOVE *A so-called 'pull-along' doll marked 'Germany 7' on the head. He has a wood-and-wire body and painted wooden limbs and is 25 cm/10 in tall. The wooden base is trimmed with painted paper. As the toy is pulled, the wheel movement causes the boy to turn his head and whip the sheep. Although the head is German, the toy was made for the French market. (Granny's Goodies, London).*

LEFT AND BELOW *Clockwork swimming doll perfected by Charles Bertran, Paris, and produced by M. Martin automation maker and called 'Ondine'. Head marked 'Halbig S & H 2½'. She performs the breast stroke; her cork body makes her buoyant and a metal casing protects the machinery. Wooden limbs and metal hands and all original swimming outfit probably by Au Nain Bleu. (Collection — Mr. and Mrs. Austin Smith, Avon).*

RIGHT *Bisque-headed open mouth doll, 60 cm/24 in high, the head marked 'A 15 Paris' and in red 'Le Parisien'. She has fixed blue eyes, jointed composition body and a key wind mechanism which activates her legs to walk. She has good face painting, pierced ears and original purple carton head pate. (Granny's Goodies, London).*

BELOW *Back of head which reads 'A-15 Paris' incised and in red 'Le Parisien'.*

## MUSICAL AUTOMATA

Roullet & Decamps was a famous French firm whose name the collector of automata will come to revere. M. Jean Roullet was renowned for his performing characters and animals produced between 1865 and 1910 at his workshop at 10 Rue du Parc, Paris. With his son-in-law Ernest Decamps, who became his partner, he began producing a wealth of very fine automata. The earlier mechanism of, for instance, the negro flute player

or the monkey conjuror were perhaps later adapted: they usually used Simon & Halbig or Jumeau heads and were probably the originators of the famous 'Jumeau *Magicienne*' ('Lady Magician') or 'Le Cerisier' ('The Cherry Seller'), 'le Fumeur' ('The Smoker'), the 'Mexican', 'la Marquise', 'la Japonaise', 'la Fillette Piano', and many, many more. Another famous Decamps walking doll is the nursemaid pushing a baby in a baby carriage and there is also the rabbit which appears from the heart of a cabbage.

Yet another notable name in the world of automata, and again French, was the name of H & G Vichy (1862-1890) carrying on business at 36 Rue Montmorency. Many very fine examples of their craftsmanship remain today. The best known Vichy automaton is probably the 'Pierrot Serenading the Moon' in which Pierrot sits with his musical instrument on one hand of a moon figure with eyes, nose and mouth. It is hard to believe that these wonderful extravagances were really toys in the most understood sense of the word for they would have appealed more to the adult than to the child.

Marotte dolls can sometimes be found with a great variety of bisque heads. The word 'Marotte' means a stick with a doll's head dressed in a fancy hat at one end. A Marotte is simply a head and plump upper torso, and is not a whole doll. With these dolls, the stick is held and swung round and round to activate a musical box beneath the head.

## Collecting Musical Dolls And Automata

◆ **LIMITED BUDGET DOLLS** Generally speaking, unless you are extremely lucky you will not find a doll in the lower price range. Musical dolls and automata are rare and desirable which means they are also expensive.

◆ **MEDIUM PRICE DOLLS** Good examples of Autoperipatetikos dolls, with various heads, appear not to have increased too much in value over the years, and may be found in this price category. Some 'pull toys' appear to be reasonably priced in spite of their relative scarcity, as do marottes and some dolls with simple walking mechanisms.

◆ **TOP PRICE RANGE DOLLS** These are the dolls with numerous functional movements and fine bisque heads, notably Jumeau dolls with closed mouths. Collectors will pay highly for fine examples; condition of costume and movement determine prices to some extent. Fine examples of dolls by famous makers, in good condition and with early dates are also at the top end of the range in this area of collecting.

LEFT *Rare Roullet & Decamps musical automaton of Pierrot and the Moon, French (c.1890). The papier mâché full moon has a painted face with open mouth and tongue which lustly moves from side to side and fixed brown glass paperweight eyes. (Courtesy Sotheby's, London).*

# CLOTH DOLLS

From a child's point of view, the warmth and cuddliness of cloth dolls makes them especially attractive. Cloth, or rag, dolls have been with us since the earliest times: they have been found in the ancient tombs of Peru and Egypt.

A rag doll was always an affordable toy. It could be either homemade or commercially produced and was within reach of both rich and poor. Some cloth dolls were made purely as playthings, others were produced for promotional purposes. Promotional dolls are a collecting field in themselves and include such dolls as 'Rastus, Cream of Wheat Chef' (1922) or the two-piece rag dolls Kelloggs 'Goldilocks and the Mama Bear' (1917-18) designed by Lela Fellom and the 'Aunt Jemima' doll (1923-1925).

## Leading Manufacturers Of Cloth Dolls

Certain companies' names spring to mind when considering cloth dolls, among them Käthe Kruse and Lenci, both with an inspiring history of manufacture and still in business today. Such names as Steiff, Chad Valley, Deans Rag Book Company and Nora Wellings were also in the forefront. Besides these wellknown firms' products, there are numerous cloth dolls and advertising dolls from anonymous companies.

## Käthe Kruse

Käthe Kruse was born in 1883 in Breslau, Silesia. She had a large family and a great love of children and since she was an artist and her husband a sculptor, she used her own children as models for her very realistic dolls, the first of which were made for them. Her early commissioned dolls were made in Berlin (from 1910) and the later ones in Bavaria.

To make the dolls, the head was first sculpted and a mould taken. The shape of the head was made from stiffened muslin which was sprayed with fixative and painted. In the early dolls the finely grained muslin was visible.

Sometimes the painting on these dolls has been chipped off or worn away, but unless it is extremely bad, it is best left alone. Overpainting is usually rated against a doll in terms of value. A doll in

RIGHT *Cloth doll, 47.5 cm/19 in tall with painted eyes and real hair lashes, felt body and felt clothing. A Lenci lookalike. To her right is a cloth doll by Chad Valley. She has a velvet body, blond mohair wig, glass eyes (rare in a cloth doll) a felt hat and matching dress and shoes. (Collection Jerie Leslie – U.S.A.).*

RIGHT *Pair of Käthe Kruse dolls. The boy has a painted face and painted brown hair. The girl is signed on the left foot and numbered in red '13449'. (Author's collection.)*

RIGHT *Ballerina doll made of plush fabric with moulded face and 1920s-style face painting and exotic eye shadowing and highly-rouged cheeks. She is 57.5 cm/23 in tall and is dressed in her original net tutu. Her pointed toes are in felt ballet shoes. (Collection - Naomi Gerwat-Clark).*

poor facial condition is priced accordingly. Since the Käthe Kruse firm is still in operation it is possible to send dolls back to the factory for repair and renovation, but repair means different things to different people and the collector is recommended to proceed with extreme caution before taking any decisions regarding restoration. Paint chips, facial scratches and rubbed noses are common, but such wear is acceptable and should be left alone. After all, these dolls were toys, designed to be loved and played with, and a few signs of wear should not cause anxiety. A toy in mint condition, on the other hand, may denote one that was unsold or unsuccessful, inasmuch as it was not played with.

The early Käthe Krüse dolls have appealingly sad faces, and it is said that she made them like that to reflect the sadness of the 1914-1918 war years. These dolls were not cheap to begin with and they command good prices today, particularly the earlier ones. During World War I and after, the materials used in manufacture changed, and the factory began producing shop mannequins: these large dolls have become costly and are extremely collectable.

Her dolls are signed Käthe Kruse on the left foot and are marked with a serial number. This was a coded control number system from which the age

of the doll can be ascertained if it has not worn off. Between 1945 and 1951 the right foot bore the stamp 'Made in Germany US Zone'. At first, Käthe Kruse dolls were made under contract by Kämmer & Reinhardt (1910) but these examples, in production for only a year or so, are rare.

Until 1928 Käthe Kruse dolls had loosely sewn-on heads; the turned head was first produced in 1929. From 1910-29 they all had painted hair after which real hair wigs were introduced and became very popular, although the painted hair examples still continued. The eyes were almost always painted, and all dolls had closed mouths. One dating clue is that dolls made before 1930 had very wide hips, after which they were narrower.

## Doll Types

It is interesting to note that from 1910-1956 only five different doll head types were produced, with slight variations as well as different numbers and names. The first head was merely called no. 1. second was 'Schlenkerchen' ('The Little Dawdler') — Doll II 'Träumerchen' ('The Little Dreamer') and 'Du Mein' ('You mine'). Dolls V and VI were next (Dolls III and IV did not exist.) 'Deutsches Kind' ('German Child') was Doll VIII and 'Hämpelchen' was Doll XII. After the 1957 model, Hanne Kruse dolls came into existence. Käthe Kruse dolls were also produced in celluloid. The firm's financial crisis of 1950 led to the production of synthetic doll heads. Old style heads were also produced and also magnesit heads, made from a cement-like substance.

Käthe Kruse died in 1968 at the age of 85, but her memory lives on in her creations, and her dolls continue to be made in West Germany in Donauwörth.

## LENCI DOLLS (1920)

Lenci dolls are to Italy what Käthe Kruse dolls are to Germany. Similarly, they began early, and continue production today. "Lenci" was the pet name of Elena, wife of Enrico di Scavini of Turin who made felt dolls of extremely high quality and design. They were first registered under the Lenci trade mark in 1922. The dolls appeal to people of all ages and early examples are highly valued by collectors.

Lenci dolls are characterised by their all-felt heads and bodies with articulated limbs, painted features and exquisitely designed felt clothes. The faces were moulded with great realism and child-like expression, with chubby cheeks. Sometimes the clothes are of patchwork, with felt floral trims. Some of the child dolls have cross expressions; some are girl or lady dolls, their faces painted with two-tone lips; their eyes often have two white dots added; some have real hair wigs and others mohair. It is popularly believed that the Lenci hands have the two middle fingers stitched together but this is erroneous: some are like this but others have only stitched finger definition. Because of the commercial success of Lenci dolls there were many copies at the time. True Lencis are marked in numerous ways — with ink stamps, card tags, ribbon labels and metal tags — the earliest being the metal tag. After 1938, cardboard tags were used. The firm produced a great variety of dolls including a complete series of foreign costume dolls, a range of ethnic and sporting dolls, miniatures and mascots, as well as the well-loved child dolls.

Lenci dolls were always quite expensive and certain serial numbers of doll attract a higher price than others due to general appeal. Condition and original clothing, as always, are determining factors in price: these dolls were particularly known for their colourful felt clothes. Unfortu-

LEFT *Four Lenci dolls. The large blonde doll on the far left dates from 1930. She has a black Lenci stamp on the left foot, a pressed felt face and eyes looking right. She wears her original cream net dress. She is nearly 42.5 cm/17 in tall. The large doll to her right also dates from 1930. She is 62.5 cm/25 in tall with swivel head, open-closed mouth and simulated teeth and a long black mohair wig in a snood. Her felt clothing is original. The doll on the far right whose eyes are looking to one side has a black mohair wig and swivel hips. She is 45 cm/18 in tall. The little girl doll on the right has a Lenci Torino paper label and a Bresse label. She stands 22.5 cm/9 in tall and holds a felt cockerel in her arms. To her left stands a doll with the label 'Bambola Italia Lenci Torino Made in Italy'. She is 23 cm/9½ in tall and is carrying a mohair-covered duck with orange beak and feet. (Courtesy Sotheby's - London).*

nately, they are subject to moth and other infestations, and signs of insect damage should not be ignored. Dolls can be treated for such problems and careful repair to holes undertaken but this is difficult and the inclusion of an infested doll in an otherwise healthy collection could have serious results. The most highly prized Lenci dolls are those made between 1920 and 1930.

## STEIFF DOLLS (1877)

Fräulein Margarete Steiff, Giengen, Württemburg, Germany is best known for stuffed toy animals of superior quality. Although she died in 1909, the firm continued in the family and is still going today. Her dolls were of felt, plush and velvet and were characterized by a seam down the centre of the face (which gives a rather odd appearance) and a button in the ears. Felt head dolls were first made in 1894. Most were character dolls which have become extremely hard to find. Some have specially balanced feet enabling them to stand up without support.

## COLLECTING CLOTH DOLLS – WHERE TO START

**LIMITED BUDGET DOLLS** Some of the English cloth dolls used to be reasonably inexpensive and easier to find, but recent increases in the price of the Lenci dolls appear to have affected the prices of English cloth dolls as they have a similar appeal and charm. Condition determines value in the final analysis.

**MIDDLE OF THE RANGE DOLLS** Some of the later Käthe Kruse dolls may come into this category, as well as those in poorer condition, and some of the less sought-after numbers in the series of Lenci dolls.

**TOP OF THE RANGE DOLLS** Among the most costly of the cloth dolls are the Steiff dolls, early Lencis and early examples by Käthe Kruse, particularly the 'Sand Baby', made as a hospital training doll. Prices have increased rapidly in the last few years.

# CELLULOID DOLLS

Celluloid was originally a patent name, but it has now become accepted as a term for the pre-plastic material from which some 'unbreakable' dolls were made, although, in fact, it was quite brittle and very breakable. In 1869, in the USA, the Hyatt brothers patented a nitrocellulose and camphor substance which they called 'celluloid', which can be considered as the first synthetic material. In fact, the substance had been created earlier in England. The invention of celluloid had a revolutionary effect on the average household, and ivory and wooden items such as combs and toothbrushes now gave way to moulded celluloid ones. Sheets of celluloid could be moulded and compressed under heat and finely detailed dolls' heads could be produced.

It is a common misconception that celluloid dolls are late in date. The Rheinische Gummi und Celluloid Fabrik Co. in Germany was producing dolls in 1873 and their tortoise or 'Schildkröte' trademark, without the diamond, was registered in 1889, so many of these dolls are indeed earlier than is often supposed. In 1899, the same firm used the tortoise in the diamond with the words 'Schutzmarke' (trademark) beneath.

Until the last few years, celluloid was always considered the poor relation of the doll world, but nowadays it is avidly collected, particularly by Germans. By the early years of this century many firms were involved in celluloid toy manufacturing and its non-peeling or flaking properties were very attractive. However, there were as many disadvantages as there were advantages in the material, and these eventually led to its decline and to the production of what we now know as plastic. Celluloid proved to be fragile and flammable; if it was too thin it would squash, and if too thick it would crack; it would become bleached and brittle in the sunlight. However, with all these problems it is surprising how many examples one still finds of dolls intact and in remarkably good condition. It is likely that cracked and damaged examples found their way to rubbish tips and perished, unlike their bisque counterparts some of which lay buried for nearly 100 years, to be dug up again from Victorian rubbish tips and reloved in the 1970s and 80s. The popularity of the celluloid doll declined in the 1920s and had largely disappeared by the 1930s.

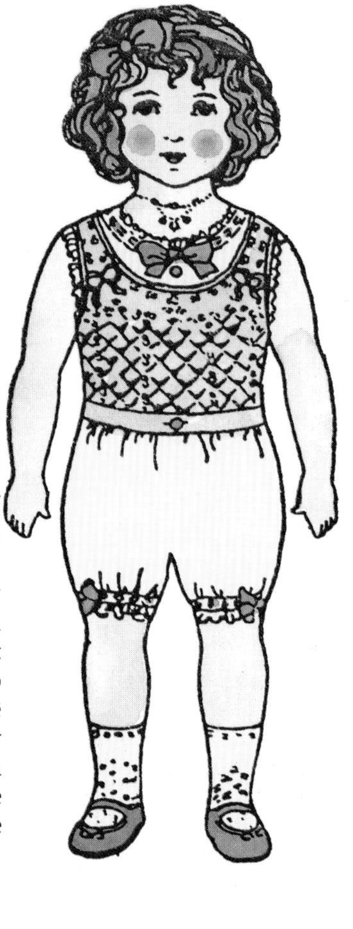

LEFT *Unusual Norah Wellings blackface doll made of brown velvet with inserted glass eyes. He is 87.5 cm/35 in tall and has a black mohair wig stitched to the head. Fingers are individual except for the centre ones which are stitched together. He wears an amber bead necklace. (Grannie's Goodies, London).*

LEFT *French celluloid doll, 52.5 cm/21 in tall. The head and back are marked 'Tête de l'aigle' (Eagle Head) and bear the symbol of Petitcolin of Paris and the inscription 'France 57½'. The moulded 1920s hairstyle dates the doll.*

## CELLULOID DOLLMAKERS

One of the most exciting things about collecting celluloid dolls, apart from the fact that inexpensive examples are still relatively easy to find, is that many renowned doll manufacturing companies in both Germany and America made celluloid examples of their bisque-headed dolls; these bear the same mould numbers and are obviously much less expensive than their bisque look-alikes. They are, on the other hand, more sought-after than the basic celluloid baby doll and command higher prices. They are often on the same quality bodies as the bisque heads. It is also probable that during the years in which the dolls' hospitals existed, many dolls had broken bisque heads replaced by celluloid which was cheaper and less fragile.

Among others, celluloid heads have been found with the marks of Armand Marseille, Kestner, Jumeau and K * R; some of the better mould numbers of the K * R characters are made of celluloid and are quite rare. America's Bye-Lo baby has also been found in celluloid. Prior to World War II, the Japanese made a great variety of celluloid dolls, and celluloid Kewpies and mechanical dolls from America were also produced. The German firm of Käthe Kruse made celluloid dolls as well as a whole new range of costume dolls; König & Wernicke of Waltershausen made celluloid dolls in 1912 as did Bruno Schmidt in 1900. Although the finest celluloid dolls are from the well-known doll manufacturers in France, Germany and the USA, they have been made all over the world.

Among the French celluloid dolls, the most commonly found marks are SNF in a diamond (Société Nobel Francaise, registered in 1939 and in 1960) and SIC in a diamond (Société Industrielle du Celluloid), and the Eagle symbol and the word 'France' (made by Petitcolin 1902-1925). The early celluloids very much resembled the pale flesh tones of the bisque dolls, while later examples developed stronger colouring.

By far the rarest of the celluloid dolls is the celluloid resin of the French fashion type swivel-head doll, usually to be found on a leather body. Nothing is clearly known or documented about these dolls and they may even be American. The only certainty is that they are almost never found. Some celluloid dolls have real hair wigs while others have moulded hair in contemporary styles which give a more accurate historical reference.

Celluloid heads are to be found on all-celluloid bent limb baby bodies, on jointed composition bodies, on leather bodies with U-joint thighs, straight-limb toddler bodies or fixed limbs. Eyes may be painted, made of glass or even celluloid. Some celluloid dolls are very crude while others are as fine in quality as the bisque dolls.

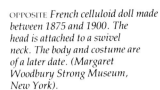

OPPOSITE *French celluloid doll made between 1875 and 1900. The head is attached to a swivel neck. The body and costume are of a later date. (Margaret Woodbury Strong Museum, New York).*

LEFT *German Kämmer & Reinhardt doll with celluloid head and composition body, wearing original checked pinafore dress. Made some time between 1905 and 1927. (Margaret Woodbury Strong Museum, New York).*

## COLLECTING CELLULOID DOLLS – WHERE TO START

◆ **LIMITED BUDGET** There is a wealth of celluloid costume dolls from various countries to be found, and because they appear not to be very commercial they are quite inexpensive. In addition, baby dolls with all-celluloid bodies and limbs, made both in France and Germany in the 1920s and 1930s are fairly easy to find and, although they are not expensive they have doubled in price over the last five years, and are obviously becoming more collectable. Celluloid heads without bodies are sometimes considered collectable, as well as celluloid toddler dolls with moulded hair or wigs, and with either all-celluloid bodies or the more usual, earlier, composition bodies.

◆ **MEDIUM RANGE** Most of the well-known bisque doll manufacturers made celluloid counterparts sometimes bearing the bisque doll mould numbers. These are much sought after. For example, a rare character mould number Kämmer & Reinhardt doll which may sell for several thousand pounds in bisque may be available in celluloid for only a fraction of the price. They are found on both composition and leather bodies, while the later examples may have leatherette bodies.

French celluloid dolls which are unmarked or not particularly fine are also in the medium range, as are dolls from countries such as Poland and Japan.

◆ **TOP QUALITY** Almost impossible to find, and priced accordingly, is the French fashion type, or Jumeau, doll in celluloid.

# ENGLISH DOLLS

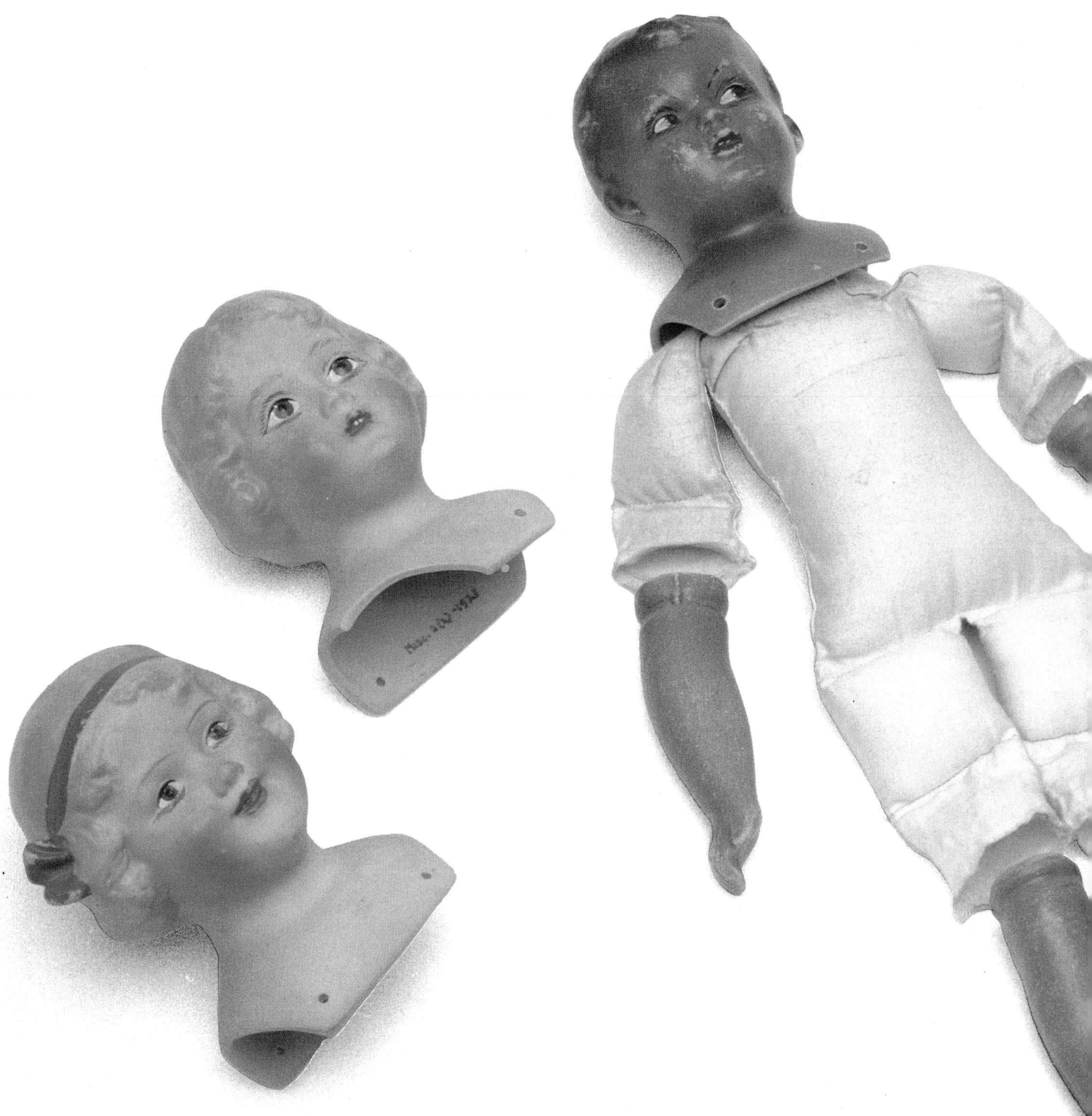

BELOW *Interchangeable heads made by the Doll Pottery Company (1915/22) in 1916 and bearing the design registration numbers together with D.P. Co. There are three stoneware heads, two sets of stoneware limbs and one cloth body. (Bethnal Green Museum of Childhood).*

RIGHT *Classic doll made by Speights Ltd. of Dewsbury (1913-24). The shoulder head is stoneware, the body cloth and the limbs composition, with poor quality mohair wig. Mark on back of shoulder plate: 4. CLASSIC ENGLAND. (Bethnal Green Museum of Childhood).*

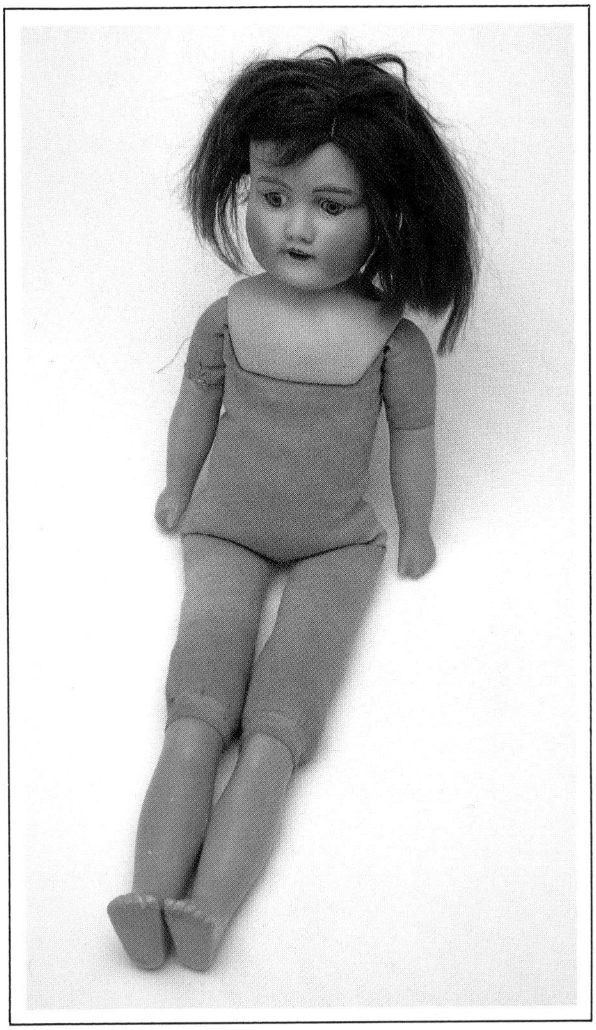

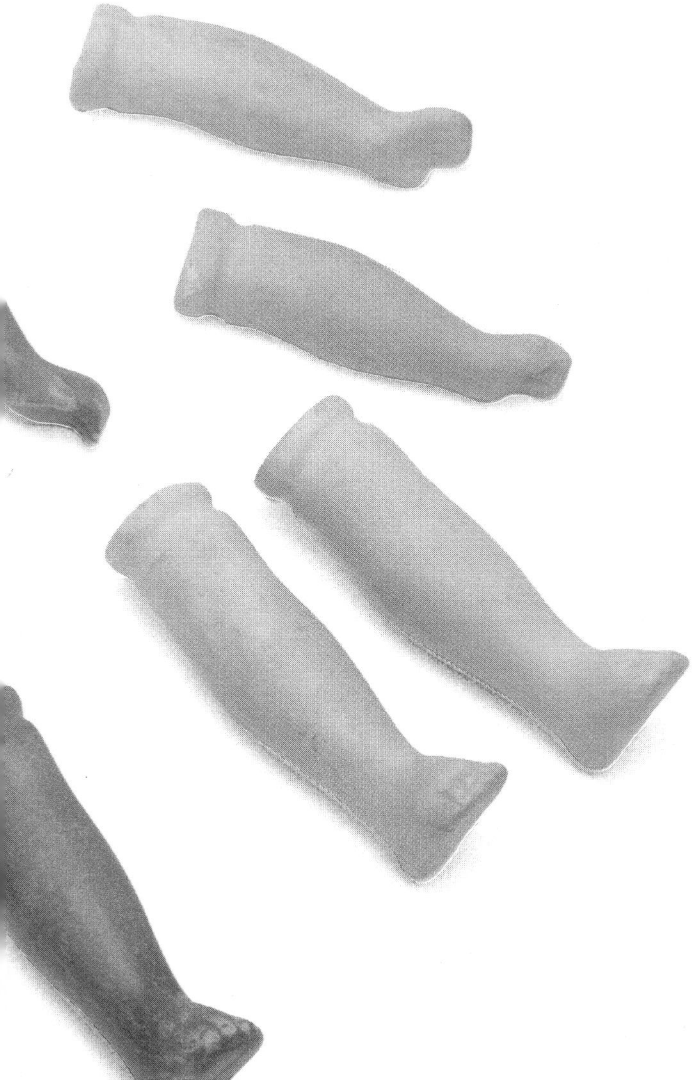

With the ban on imports of German toys in the 1914-18 War period, English companies attempted to produce pottery-headed dolls for the home market. The industry was developed in a very short time, and the dolls were crude, of poor quality, and generally unattractive. However, since they were produced for such a limited period — virtually until the lifting of the ban on importation — they are rare and probably worth collecting. Many British doll companies existed over the period, producing wood, wax, china or pottery and fabric dolls. They are too numerous for all to be mentioned in this book, but some of the most popular appear to have been the following:

Diamond Pottery Co. Ltd., Stoke-on-Trent. This company was affiliated to a hard-paste porcelain company and most of the English china headed dolls to be found will have the D.P.C. mark. This may also be attributable to the Doll Pottery Co., who used a great variety of marks and were in operation between 1916 and 1922 in Staffordshire. The quality of these Diamond dolls is usually

crude, with poor painting and highly-coloured, pinkish bisque, although some good examples exist. The Diamond doll industry petered out around 1940 and the company then became the Diamond Tile Co., producing tiles. The Doll Pottery Co., Ltd. (1915-1922) produced possibly the greatest variety of dolls and doll heads, and in numerous sizes — shoulder heads, moulded hair dolls, girl and boy babies, clowns, negroes and pierrots.

W. H. Goss & Co. 1858-1944, of Staffordshire, produced limbs and heads with painted and glass eyes. These dolls are now extremely rare and although they appear somewhat crude and highly-coloured in comparison with the German and French dolls, they do command quite high prices. Goss is normally associated with commemorative china ware, and not dolls.

Hancock & Sons (1857-1937). By 1917 this firm was producing over 70 different types of dolls' heads — open and closed mouth, moulded-haired, and so on. As with the other English companies, face painting and detail was crude. There were many other English porcelain companies making dolls at this period, but few of their products are marked or identifiable.

LEFT *One of the finest examples of a boudoir doll ever found by the Author. She is 102.5 cm/41 in tall with stockinette, painted face in almost mint condition, stencilled eyes, cloth body and limbs jointed at knees and elbows. Tiny waist, large bust and exquisite all original clothes, underwear, satin dress, diamanté- and-lace trims, original bonnet with floral organza decoration and flowers and original high-heeled shoes. (Author's collection).*

ABOVE *HMS Furious Sailor by Chad Valley about 1935 to a design by Norah Wellings of dark blue velvet. These sailor dolls were sold as souvenirs on ocean-going liners. (Bethnal Green Museum of Childhood).*

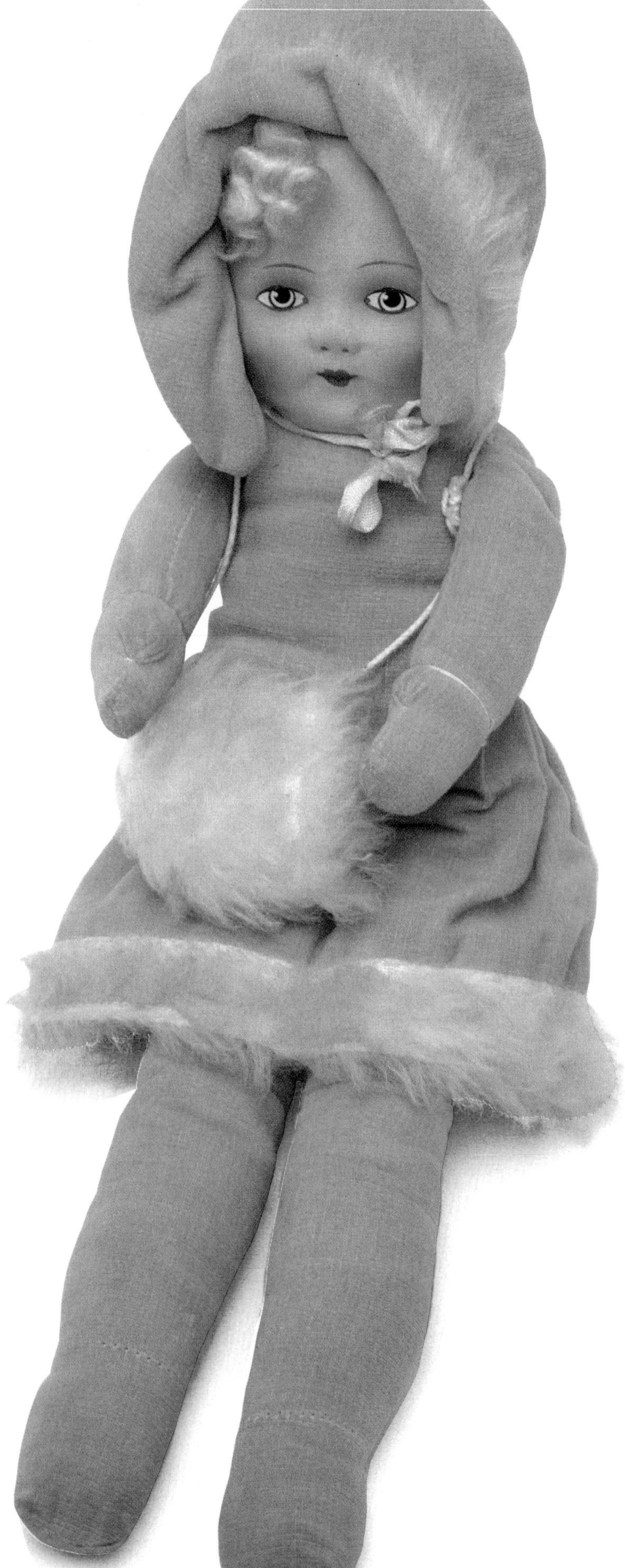

## FABRIC DOLLS

There were a great many manufacturers of English fabric dolls and the most significant names were inevitably the most prolific; it is their work that is likely to be found by the modern collector.

Boudoir dolls are not highly sought-after commercially, but some very attractive examples can be found in the cheaper range of dolls. As always, condition determines value. Obviously the more elaborate the costume, the more costly the doll may be. Boudoir dolls, as the name suggests, were designed to adorn the boudoir or bedroom. They usually took the form of long-limbed women with fabric- or silk-covered and painted faces, often with hats and decorative costumes made by different designers. They were made between 1910 and 1938 by such firms as Chad Valley and Dean's Rag Book Co.

Chad Valley Dolls, founded in 1823 and still going strong, was a Birmingham firm specializing in promotional dolls and toys of well-known characters and cartoons, such as Bonzo dog. They also made Teddy Bears and stuffed animals of high quality, and were toy makers to the Queen. In the 1920s they produced Mable Lucy Atwell dolls, and Snow White and the Seven Dwarfs, in all of which the quality of workmanship showed. Sometimes their dolls are confused with Lenci dolls (see page 61) which command a higher price, the Chad Valley dolls still being in the lower end of the price range.

Dean & Son Ltd. London, and Dean's Rag Book Co., Ltd., its subsidiary, date back to 1840. This company has a long history of printing and publishing and is well known for its series of books in the shape of a doll. Since 1958 it has acted as sole agent for the Merrythought company and it also produces a series of national costume dolls. Dean's dolls are generally of good quality and detail — price, of course, is governed by condition — but they are in the lower end of the price range for cloth dolls. They are to be recommended as an area for the new collector to explore. It is as well to remember that it can be worth while to purchase the latest products of companies such as this: today's new dolls are tomorrow's antiques.

Both of these companies frequently used felt in their doll production (as did Lenci Dolls). Originally made from beaver or rabbit hair, and latterly from wool waste, felt could be steamed into shape, and it could be brightly-coloured. Above all, it was hard wearing. Felt did, of course, suffer from moth damage and many fine examples have been spoilt in this way. A word of caution: if you buy a

LEFT *Skater made by Dean's Rag Book Company about 1930 of pale green velvet. (Bethnal Green Museum of Childhood).*

RIGHT *Dean's Rag doll, 97.5 cm/ 39 in with clothes made on to the doll. (Granny's Goodies - London).*

SHELL
MOTOR
SPIRIT
SHELL
MOTOR
OIL
SHELL

felt doll, examine it very carefully for infestation and tell-tale holes, as a newly added doll which is infested can spread the problem to other examples in your collection. Moth damage can usually be treated and the doll made safe.

Nora Wellings Dolls (1926-1959) was established by an ex-Chad Valley designer in Shropshire. She is perhaps best known for the little tourist sailor dolls made to sell on board ship. Apart from her felt dolls, Nora Wellings is perhaps most often associated with velvet dolls of very high quality. These are usually marked and are still relatively inexpensive by doll standards.

## ENGLISH WAX DOLLS

England is perhaps most highly regarded for its wax dolls, and among makers several are outstanding: Charles and William Marsh 1865-1913 made wax and wax-over-papier-mâché dolls, and the Meech brothers 1865-1891, made wax dolls by royal appointment. The most famous of the English wax doll makers was perhaps Madame Augusta Montanari who died in 1864, the business being carried on by her son Richard, and the manufacture of Montanari dolls appears from all the directories to be between 1850 and 1887. Mrs Lucy Peck (1846-1930) was another well-known name of the period, but the best generally-known wax doll or figure maker today is of course Madame Marie Tussaud (1760-1850). Mention of her must be made as most members of the public have been to the famous London waxworks which bears her name and which she founded, although few of her actual works remain, most having been destroyed in the fire of 1925. She was not so much a doll maker as a figure maker, and although she certainly made dolls, they are hardly ever found. Tussaud is known for her portrait wax dolls, but wax babies are documented as having been made by her. Pierotti is among the most famous names in wax doll manufacture: the Pierottis were an amazing family of wax doll makers from 1770 onwards, through successive generations. The last Pierotti doll maker retired in 1935.

## WOODEN DOLLS

These are generally very early, and some fine examples exist, but they are nearly always priced beyond the reach of the novice collector. We have very little historical detail about the manufacture of wooden dolls, but they are likely to have been made by small craftsmen, perhaps furniture makers or turners, who would have had suitable tools for turning the wooden stumps. Few examples date from before the late 17th century. The most famous of all English wooden dolls are Lord and Lady Clapham, a pair documented as

RIGHT *Mother Goose's Rag Book printed on linen by Dean's Rag Book Company about 1916. The illustrations are by Hilda Cowham who produced illustrations for the magazine Home Chat. (Bethnal Green Museum of Childhood).*

No 201 DEAN'S RAG BOOKS. Patented.
MOTHER GOOSE'S RAG BOOK
I saw a ship a-sailing, a-sailing on the sea;
And, oh! it was all laden with pretty things for thee.
There were comfits in the cabin and apples in the hold;
The sails were made of silk, and the masts were made of gold.
And Johnny shall go to the fair,
And Johnny shall have a new ribbon,
To tie up his bonny brown hair.
JAM

owned by a single family — descendants of Samuel Pepys, the diarist, who went to live in Clapham, London towards the end of his life. The dolls are unique among late 17th century examples and are in pristine condition. Lord Clapham's hat bears the label 'T. Bourdillon Hosier & Hatter to His Majesty, 14 Russel Street, Covent Garden.' They came up for auction in 1974 and, after an export licence was refused to a Swiss collector, they were eventually purchased by the Victoria & Albert Museum, where they can now be seen.

## COLLECTING ENGLISH DOLLS WHERE TO START

**LIMITED BUDGET DOLLS** English dolls are an excellent area for new collectors. They are not very widely available, but when found, the china and pottery dolls in particular are likely to be modestly priced. Watch out for quality, which tends to be poor, and should be priced accordingly. The well known makers such as Hancock and Diamond Pottery as well as the products of lesser known companies may be found. Boudoir dolls are often inexpensive: Chad Valley and Dean's Rag fabric dolls look attractive in any collection.

**MEDIUM-PRICE-RANGE-DOLLS** Goss dolls are among the rarities of the English China dolls and may be highly priced. The face painting is rather strong in colour and hot-looking, but their chief interest is in their scarcity. English wax dolls are a delight to collect and vary in price, as do the wax-over-papier-mâché with their delightful smiles and distinctive aura. The faces are generally crazed but this is part of their charm and should not be touched. Examples with fine early clothes are of particular appeal.

**TOP-OF-THE-RANGE-DOLLS** Some of the top-quality wax dolls may come into this area but it is mainly the wooden dolls which are at the top end of the category. These include examples like the almost priceless Lord & Lady Clapham, as well as early Queen Annes and those Georgian delights with their black beauty spots. There is a wide price range, starting at well above the medium band.

RIGHT *Girl in a Red Dress made by Chad Valley about 1935, a Lenci type. (Bethnal Green Museum of Childhood).*

FAR RIGHT *Lucy Peck doll made by Lucy Peck between 1902 and 1911. Though she also stamped dolls she merely repaired rather than made, this one is definitely of her manufacture. The head is poured wax and the body stuffed, mohair is inserted and the glass eyes are blue. The stamp on the body shows the 131 Regent Street address. (Bethnal Green Museum of Childhood).*

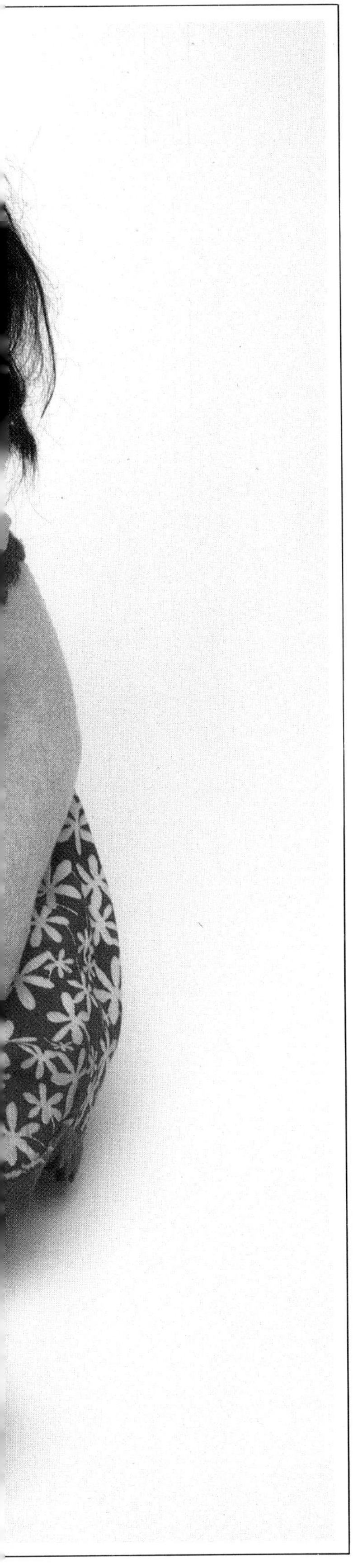

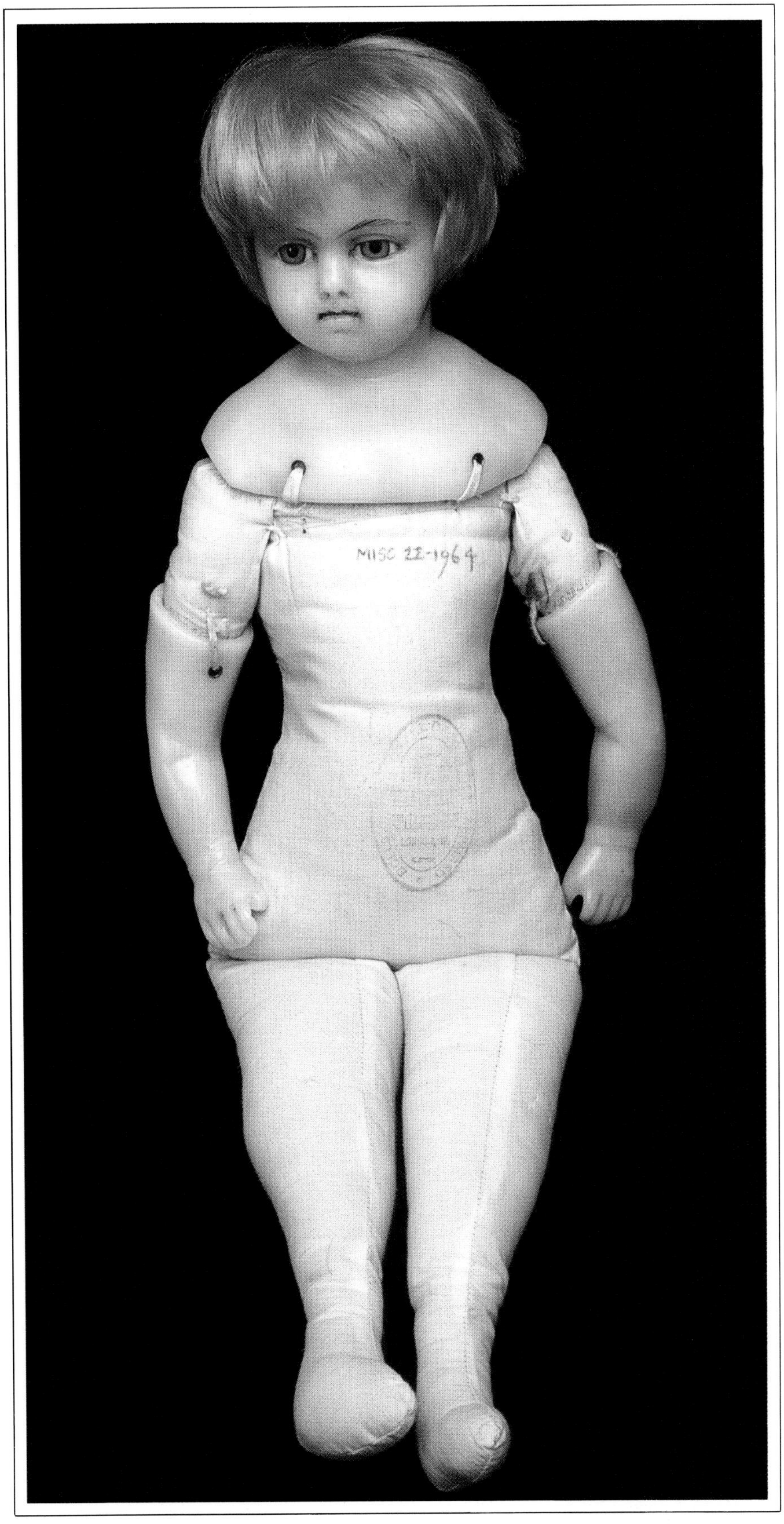
MISC 22-1964

RIGHT *Celluloid-like Baby made by the British National Dolls of London about 1955. The doll is of hard plastic. Mark on the nape of the head: BND (Bethnal Green Museum of Childhood).*

LEFT *Charles Marsh doll dating from about 1880 and dressed as a bride with a cloth body adapted to have a bust. The head is poured wax, mohair is inserted and the glass eyes are blue. There are two large body stamps including one showing the Royal Warrant. (Bethnal Green Museum of Childhood).*

RIGHT *Composition doll, 32.5 cm/13 in high. The head is marked '13 Shirley Temple'. The limbs are straight and dress and wig original. Made by the Ideal Toy Corp. N.Y., U.S.A. (1934-39). (Author's collection).*

# AMERICAN DOLLS

In the early days, the United States imported most of its dolls. American dolls are not known to have been produced before the Civil War, but later in the 19th century New York, Philadelphia and New England became the principal doll-making areas. Heads were often imported from Europe and added to American-made bodies, and at the same time many of the doll makers in America, such as Greiner had learned their skills in Europe. The best known makers of bodies were Lacmann, Steuber, Gibson and Robinson. American heads were usually of composition, papier mâché or rag, but Ernst Reinhardt, who started in Germany is thought to have made bisque heads in the United States. He settled in Philadelphia, in 1909.

LEFT *Fabric doll, 45 cm/20 in doll by Martha Chase, with painted cloth rigid arms and cloth legs, hinged at knee. She is unmarked and has painted hair rather crudely overpainted at a later period. (Collection - Naomi Gerwat-Clark).*

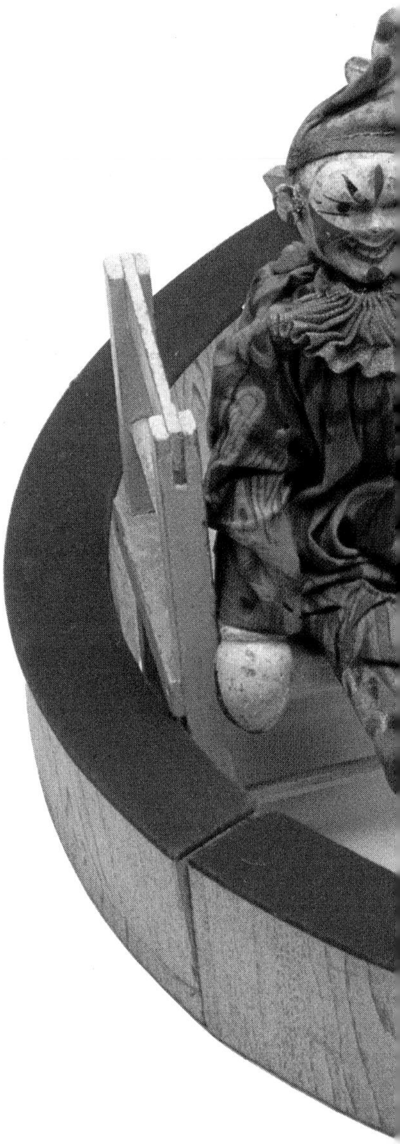

LEFT *Part of the Humpty Dumpty Circus made by A. Schoenhut & Co. in 1903. More and more characters were gradually added to the circus which first included the clowns. A Ring Master, Lion Tamer, Acrobat, Lady Acrobat and Lady Circus Rider were added and made with wooden or bisque heads. There was also a Chinaman, Hobo and Negro Dude and in 1907 Max and Moritz were introduced. A vast assortment of animals could also be added to the circus. (Author's collection).*

## PRINCIPAL DOLL MAKERS

Among the early American doll-making names is that of Izannah F. Walker of Rhode Island whose dolls are, to the inexperienced eye, somewhat like those of Martha Chase. They are made of stiffened stockinet with rather primitively painted features and painted hair, typified by corkscrew curls at the side of the head. Some have painted shoes. There is some evidence to suggest that her first dolls may have been made as early as 1840 although she did not obtain a patent until 1873. These dolls are very rare and command high prices. They are seldom, if ever, found in Europe. Izannah Walker died about 1888.

Joel Addison Hartley Ellis of Springfield, Vermont (1858-1925) is another of the early American doll makers. The early firm of Ellis, Britton & Eaton was succeeded by the Vermont Novelty Co., makers of unusual all-wooden articulated dolls known as Joel Ellis dolls. The head and body were turned in one piece and because the dolls resembled German artist's figures they were known as mannikins. They had metal hands and feet and came in three different sizes: 12, 15, and 18 in (30, 37.5 and 45 cm). The heads were pressure-moulded and hand-painted and were either blonde or brunette. These dolls are extremely rare and highly priced, and they are not generally found in Europe.

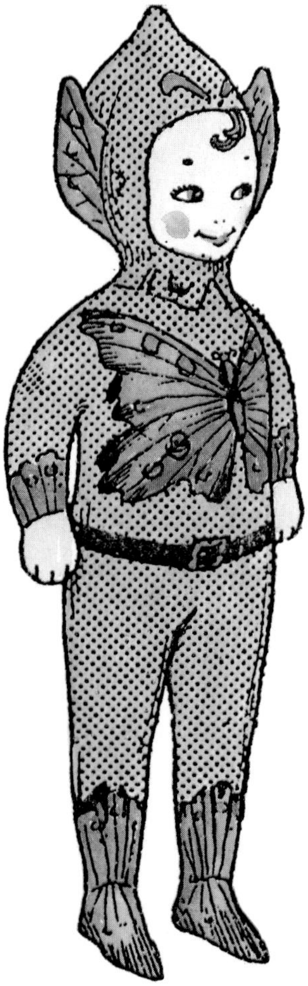

A. Schoenhut & Co. 1872-1925 of Philadelphia, made some of the most noteworthy American dolls. Albert Schoenhut was born in 1850 in Germany and, having settled in America he had great success with his Humpty Dumpty Circus in 1903. This was a wooden circus with a variety of articulating animals and circus people complete with their ladders and other apparatus. Some of the figures had bisque heads, but Schoenhut also made fully articulated wooden dolls with carved heads; some had moulded hair and others had wigs. They were strung with wire and tend to twang a little when the dolls are moved. The eyes were painted or sleeping and some of the faces resemble the K * R dolls. They are very appealing and their durability has enabled many to survive.

Arnold Print Works (1876-1925), of North Adenes, Massachusetts were manufacturers of do-it-yourself printed fabric cut-out dolls which were published for advertising purposes. The dolls were sewn and stuffed, and used to promote such names as Kelloggs and Cream of Wheat, and many others. Advertising dolls are difficult to find, probably because they have been treasured less than other types, but they have a wide appeal and cover numerous subjects: some were based on comic strip characters such as Little Orphan Annie.

Art Fabric Mills (1899-1910) New York, was

RIGHT *Rag doll, 62.5 cm/25 in, and printed on the foot 'Art Fabric Mills, New York, patented Feb 13 1900'. She has printed face, hair and hair ribbon, stuffed body with primitive stump hands and printed underwear, printed red stockings and black printed boots with laces. (Author's collection).*

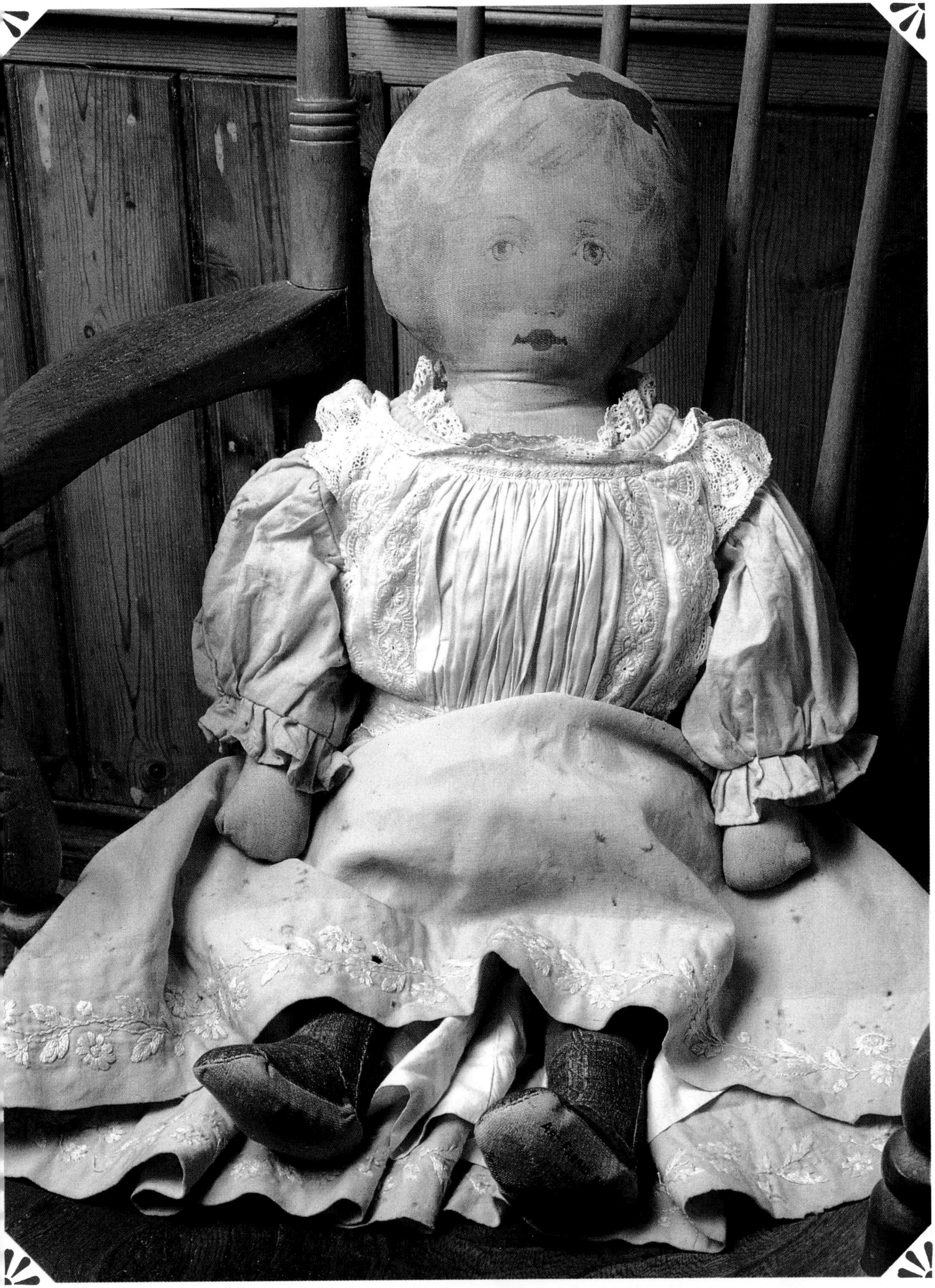

RIGHT *Old woman character doll by Bernard Ravca. The face contours are created by hand-stitching, then hand-painting. (Author's collection).*

OPPOSITE RIGHT *Character doll by Bernard Ravca, depicting an old man seated. These dolls are amongst his most popular products. (Author's collection).*

RIGHT *Two vinyl dolls by Madam Alexander. The blonde doll has a head incised '3 ALEXANDER 1979', and is known as 'Little Brother'. These dolls came as a pair and there is also a 'Little Sister'. The clothes are original. (Collection of Leona Gerwat-Clark). The dark-haired doll is a 1974 model known as 'Baby Precious'. She has vinyl limbs with well-defined moulding, stuffed body, well-rooted hair and original clothes and sleep eyes. (Collection - Naomi Gerwat-Clark).*

another fabric doll company which included black dolls in its output.

Ravca dolls are somewhat later. The French-born (1904) Bernard Ravca came to the USA in 1939 and has worked there with his wife ever since. They have produced window dolls, portraits of celebrities, royalty, sports figures, and others; they are perhaps most affectionately known for their old people character dolls.

Martha Jenks Chase 1880-1925 Pawtucket, Rhode Island formed her dolls' heads with stockinet stretched over a mask and then finished with paste and painted in oils. Ears and thumbs were applied separately and the eyes and hair (usually blonde) were painted. These dolls tend to look rather crude but have a certain realistic charm. Before 1920, the bodies were jointed at the shoulder, hips, elbows and knees, and they were said to be washable. They were marked, but in many examples the marks have worn off. Chase made some interesting dolls representing characters from Charles Dickens and Alice in Wonderland and was a prolific producer of hospital training dolls representing new-born, two-month and four-month babies, one- and four-year-old children and adults.

Louis Amberg & Son was a well-known dollmaking name in the USA, as was Madame Beatrice Alexander, whose dolls are perhaps the best loved of all American collectors' dolls. They are seldom, if ever, found in Europe and were never imported into England. Early examples fetch high prices. Madame Alexander's heritage was Russian, her father having been a doll maker from Odessa. She was his eldest daughter and she founded her own company in New York in 1923 producing rag-doll characters from Dickens. Later her company moved on to plastics and vinyls and is still producing wonderful creations to this day.

A rag version of Rose O'Neill (1909-25) was a native of Wilkes-Barre, Pennsylvania who, in 1909, designed a rag version of the universally famous Kewpie doll, later perfected and manufactured in bisque by Kestner in Germany. Many different Kewpie characters appeared in doll form.

A similar success story to that of Rose O'Neill concerns Grace Storey Putnam (1922-25), of Oakland, California. In 1922 she designed the Bye-Lo Baby doll for the Borgfeldt Doll Company. She was, at the time, a teacher in an art college, and the Bye-Lo Baby was meant to represent a real three-day-old baby. It was in fact modelled on a black baby, hence its rather negroid appearance. Bye-Lo Baby dolls are to be found in all-bisque, wax and composition, and with celluloid hands; some have curiously-shaped cloth bodies in several sizes designed by Georgene Averill. The heads were made in Germany by George Borgfeldt to whom Putnam was under contract.

RIGHT *American baby doll made in Germany by Grace Storey Putnam. The Bye-Lo baby was called the 'Million Dollar Baby' because of its vast sales. Heads were made by Kestner, Kling and Alt, Beck & Gottschalk. This head is incised 'Grace S. Putnam, Made in Germany 1360/30'. It is 32.5 cm/13 in tall. (Author's collection).*

## RUBBER DOLLS

In 1839, Charles Goodyear developed a process for making rubber less brittle which he patented in 1844, under the name vulcanization. The process involved treating rubber with sulphur, and is best known for its use in making car tyres. Charles' brother, Nelson, obtained a U.S. patent for a rubber doll's head in 1851, which was extended to 1865. The rubber dolls were attached to stuffed cloth bodies, like the papier mâché heads. They had leather crowns for the attachment of wigs.

The New York Rubber Co. and Benjamin F. Lee were just two companies that made rubber dolls under license from Goodyear. Dolls were sold through major department stores, such as Montgomery Ward.

Time has not been kind to the early rubber dolls; the paint chipped and the rubber perished. Later, the process was refined and rubber-and-composition dolls became popular. Later, only doll bodies were made from rubber.

## CELLULOID DOLLS

Celluloid dolls were also produced in the USA. In New York John Wesley and Isaiah Hyatt started manufacturing celluloid products in 1869, including some dolls. They developed the Embossing Company of New York in 1870 where they produced celluloid dolls' heads. In 1866 Franklin Darrow made raw-hide dolls' heads which closely resembled papier mâché.

## COLLECTING AMERICAN DOLLS – WHERE TO START

◆ **LIMITED BUDGET DOLLS** Advertising dolls and some of the fabric dolls may come into the lower price range. Condition is always a determining factor in this respect. Celluloid dolls are sometimes inexpensive, providing they are not celluloid versions of one of the rare character dolls with sought-after mould numbers.

◆ **MIDDLE PRICE RANGE DOLLS** These would include Bye-Lo Babies (rarely found in Europe) and Madame Alexanders, also rarely found in Europe as they were never exported.

◆ **TOP OF THE RANGE DOLLS** Generally, the very early dolls came into this category, for example Izannah Walkers, Joel Ellis dolls, Goodyear dolls & Greiners. Obviously these are very rare and therefore highly valued.

# GERMAN DOLLS

Germany was, of course, the most prolific doll-making country in the world and it is from here that doll collectors have received their greatest legacy. During their flowering the great German doll-making companies made every conceivable type of doll in a wealth of designs and materials and in great profusion. The sheer quantity produced has assured Germany's place at the forefront of the world market; although German dolls are less rare and expensive than French examples, the quality of their bisque and face painting is similarly exuberant, and their lower price is simply a reflection of the high numbers available to collectors.

The golden age of the German doll spanned roughly 75 years from the mid-19th century to the first quarter of the 20th century. During this time the Germans came to dominate the world doll market through the enormous variety of their wares and their competitive price structure. German doll-making was eventually destroyed by the world economic recession in the inter-war years, World War II, and the subsequent development of cheap synthetics in a throw-away age.

The vast majority of the German dollmakers were located in the southeastern province of Thuringia. These included — with their startup dates in parentheses — Adolf Wislizenus (1851), Alt, Beck & Gottschalck (1854), Gebrüder Krauss (1863), Edmund Ulrich Steiner (1864, later moving to the United States), Louis Wolf & Co. (1870), Bähr & Pröschild (1871), Franz Schmidt & Co. (1890), Kley & Hahn (1895), and König & Wernicke (1912).

Consequently, the town of Waltershausen gained such a reputation that wholesalers and retailers advertised "Waltershausen dolls" as a reference to the high quality of the product. Sonneburg led the reputation of being the centre for all grades of dollmaking. The dollmakers of Thuringia produced dolls not only from forestry products such as wood and papier mâché, but also from bisque and porcelain.

Since so many famous companies were located in Thuringia (now in the German Democratic Republic) there was obviously a healthy exchange of ideas, craftsmanship and even craftsmen. Furthermore, members of dollmaking families married each other temporarily merging the com-

RIGHT *Bisque-headed open mouth doll impressed 'Made in Germany 129'. Her plaster pate denotes a Kestner doll, she has delicate face painting and original wig. She is 50 cm/20 in tall with a composition jointed body. (Author's collection).*

panies, though there must also have been great rivalries.

The Thuringian lead in this field was not sudden, but grew from the labours of the early German dollmakers who established traditions of workmanship. Carvers in wood, modellers, papier mâché craftsmen and generations of cottage industry workers had built up a thriving doll and toy manufacturing tradition in South Germany. The natural resources were there in abundance — wood for carving, fine china clay, wood pulp, a dense population providing a cheap labour force, and a good transportation network, the importance of which should not be overlooked. To give some idea of the size and scale of manufacture, the firm of Fleischmann in Sonneberg, Thuringia was said to be employing some 32,000 workers, including out-workers, in 1870.

## DEVELOPMENT OF THE LEADING DOLL COMPANIES

LEFT *Bisque-headed, closed-mouth, googly-eyed doll, 17.5 cm/7 in tall with head marked 'A 253 M Nobbi Kid Reg. U.S. Pat. Germany 11/0'. She has a composition toddler-type body, original dress and later real hair wig. (Author's collection).*

Simon & Halbig of Gräfenhain, Thuringia was probably one of the first companies to develop greatly in size, and they made a profuse variety of dolls' heads in Parian and papier mâché. However, they did not make doll bodies, and when collectors say a doll is on the wrong body, this simply means that the body normally associated with that particular head at the time of sale is not now with it. Bodies were purchased from other companies and although they may be of Simon & Halbig design and produced especially for them, they were not actually made by Simon & Halbig,

ABOVE *Bisque shoulder plate doll with closed mouth, 34 cm/14 in tall. The leather body has bisque arms, fixed blue paperweight eyes and marked '139' (indistinct), probably an early Kestner made for the French doll market of the period. (Author's collection).*

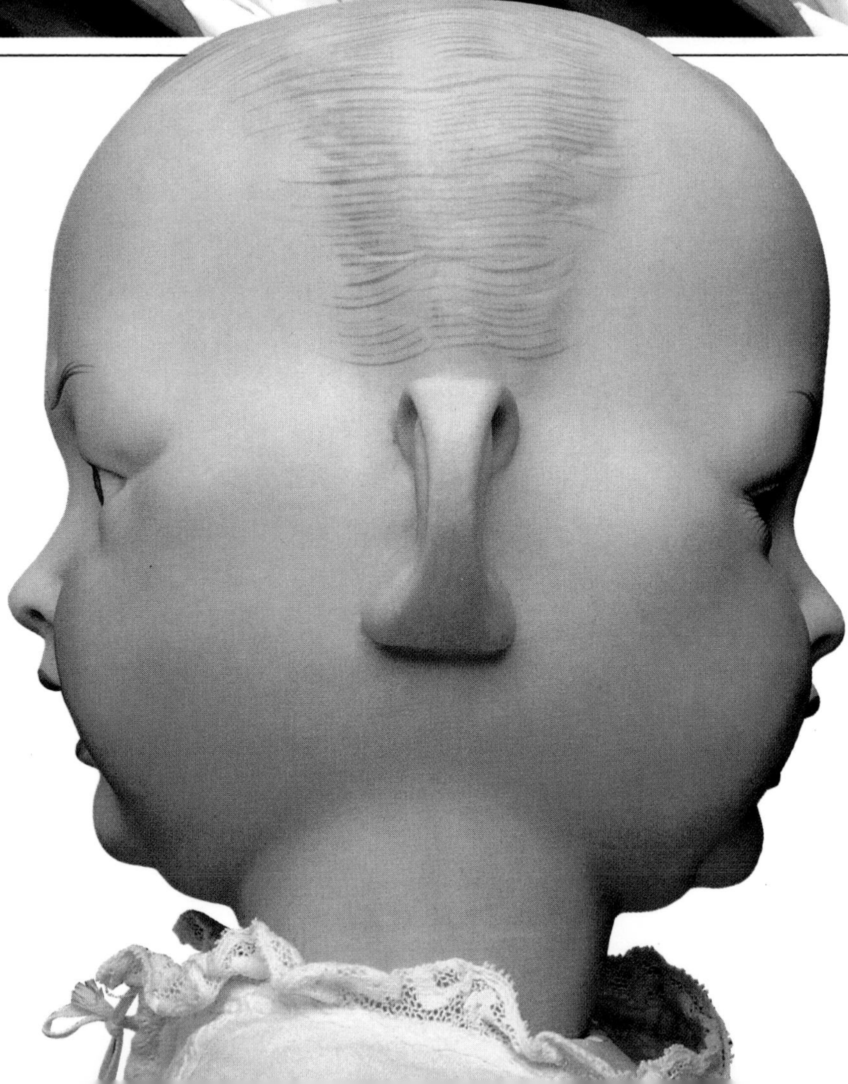

ABOVE FAR LEFT *Extremely rare two-faced bisque character baby doll. One face has an open/closed smiling mouth with moulded tongue and two painted teeth, sleeping eyes and dimples. The base of the neck is marked '12'.*

ABOVE LEFT *Other face of this two-headed bisque doll. The eyes are painted and the open/closed mouth has a moulded tongue and no teeth. The face wears an angry expression. The neck base is marked '159'.*

BELOW LEFT *Side view of the two-headed bisque doll, showing curiously thick ear.*

OVERLEAF *Fine quality open-mouth bisque headed Kämmer & Reinhardt doll with head marked 'K * R 117n', 55 cm/22 in. (Granny's Goodies - London).*

apart from the all-bisque dolls for which they did make the bodies. In fact, J. D. Kestner of Waltershausen, Thuringia was perhaps the only German company to make both their own doll heads and bodies.

It also adds to the confusion of new collectors to know that Simon & Halbig made heads for some of the renowned French factories of the period, for example Jumeau, Daspres and Roullet & Decamps. It is similar to the situation today when a cheaper item may be made in Hong Kong for an English brand name; so it was then with the French companies, who sometimes had cheaper dolls' heads made for them in Germany for assembly in France on French bodies and with French clothes.

Johannes Daniel Kestner Jr. from Waltershausen advertised his papier mâché dolls with leather bodies in 1823 though he is reputed to have started production as early as 1805. These dolls were probably the early milliners' models whose origins are obscure. He also made buttons, clothing and fine quality goods; he used the crown as his trade mark. Kestner should probably be regarded as the father of the Waltershausen doll industry: he was certainly the first in the area. His firm was probably the only company to produce both heads and bodies and therefore a Kestner doll can be regarded as a whole product of the firm and not a marriage between a head made by one firm and a body made by another. In the 1850s Kestner made china head and wax-over-papier-mâché dolls, but as these are unmarked, they cannot be identified. After Johannes Kestner died in 1859 the company bought a porcelain factory and produced Parian heads and later the bisque heads which we usually associate with Kestner. However, the Parian heads were also unmarked and are therefore not definitely identifiable. Fortunately the later, exquisite, dolls, produced from the 1880s and 1890s and onwards were marked. Kestner's grandson Adolph took over the firm in 1872 and ran it until his death in 1918, after which the company rode out World War I and the Depression, finally merging with Kämmer & Reinhardt in 1930. The company was held in extremely high esteem.

Armand Marseille (1865-1925), Köppelsdorf, Thuringia, is probably the first doll manufacturer's name which the new collector will learn, for 'A & M' dolls have always been regarded as some of the least expensive of the German dolls and therefore the most likely purchases for the new collector. Armand Marseille's company was the most prolific of the doll makers and his quality of production was consistently excellent. Because of the laws of supply and demand, the most commonly found dolls are among the least expensive and because such huge numbers of A & M dolls were made, they are the most frequently

encountered by modern collectors. Marseille was born in Russia in 1856 and later settled near Sonneberg where he started business as a porcelain factory. By 1890, he was producing bisque heads and began, with his son Armand Marseille Jnr. to supply heads to George Borgfeldt, Louis Wolf, Charles Bergmann and others. Armand Marseille Jnr. married the daughter of Ernst Heubach, a dollmaker who began manufacturing in 1887. The Marseille company, like many others, suffered during the War years of 1914-18 when dolls were not exported from Germany, the USA or the rest of Europe. However, by 1920 they were in production again and remained so until about 1925.

RIGHT AND BELOW RIGHT *Rare bisque-headed Simon & Halbig doll 52.5 cm/21 in with head marked 'SH 1039 Dep'. She has very large eyes which are fixed but which appear to sleep as the metal, wax-covered eyelids are opened and closed by a curious movement operated by two strings which come through the back of the head. She is all original and has a composition jointed body. (Author's collection).*

BELOW LEFT *This the back of the head of the K * R character doll on page 108. It is incised 'K * R Simon & Halbig 117'.*

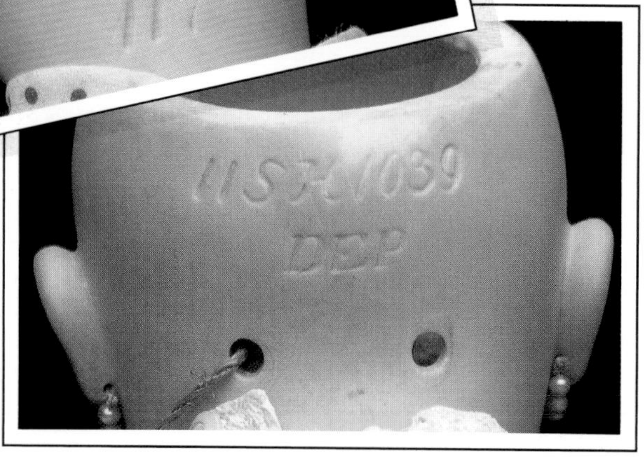

Gebrüder Heubach, of Lichte, Thuringia, founded in 1820, was one of the earlier doll manufacturing companies in Germany. This firm is primarily noted for its character dolls, 'Piano Babies', figurines and all-bisque dolls. Many had moulded hair and intaglio eyes and were of good quality, although the standard of the bodies varied. The intaglio painted eyes had moulded details, including a raised white dot. In most cases, the pupil and iris were indented to give a deeper look, and this gave the Heubach eyes a realism and range of expression possible with glass eyes. Moulded hair may have been adopted for cheapness or it may have been a throwback to the moulded-haired Parians. The Gebrüder Heubach dolls are usually marked with a rising sun or 'Heubach' in a square. Some collectors confuse Gebrüder Heubach with Ernst Heubach whose firm was founded in 1887. The Ernst Heubach dolls are generally marked 'Heubach, Köppelsdorf', EH or HK, sometimes with a horse-shoe trade mark. Four and five digit numbers seem to have been used for Gebrüder Heubach but their earlier dolls, before the period of their character dolls, are something of a mystery because the numbering is inconsistent, often unaccompanied by a symbol and sometimes in such an obscure position on the doll's body that it cannot be located, for instance, under a shoulder where the body would hide it. It is known that Heubach produced 'dolly-faced' dolls before the character dolls which were such a distinctive feature of their output.

It is confusing to learn that such famous doll-producing firms as Franz and Bruno Schmidt, Heinrich Handwerck, Kämmer & Reinhardt, Bergmann, König and Wernicke, Kley & Hahn and Catterfelder-Puppenfabrik, to name a few, did not make their own doll heads. Times changed, and by about 1927 the Kämmer & Reinhardt firm had take over production of the Simon & Halbig heads. Heads can often be found with both the K * R and the Simon & Halbig marks on them: the six-sided star was adopted as a symbol by the Kämmer & Reinhardt factory. Simon & Halbig heads were also produced for mechanical dolls, novelty items and bisque-faced dolls, and this was probably the first firm to use coloured bisque for black dolls and Burmese dolls with slanted eyes. Chinese and Red Indian dolls were also produced with appropriate bisque colouring.

The firm of Kämmer & Reinhardt of Waltershausen is a famous name in the doll-collecting field and is best known for its character dolls. These are perhaps the *crême-de-la crême* of the German doll industry, certainly in terms of price, rarity and collectability. The firm began in around 1886. Ernst Kämmer was an experienced doll-maker but it is not known who made the Kämmer & Reinhardt heads at that time. Certainly Simon & Halbig made them after 1902 when Ernst died. Kämmer & Reinhardt developed new stringing methods for doll's bodies. Any improvement had to be patented, because with so much competition ideas would be copied immediately if an invention was not patented. It is from this wealth of patent material that we have gleaned so much of our doll information. Mr. Kämmer claimed to be the first to cut an opening into the doll's mouth and insert teeth.

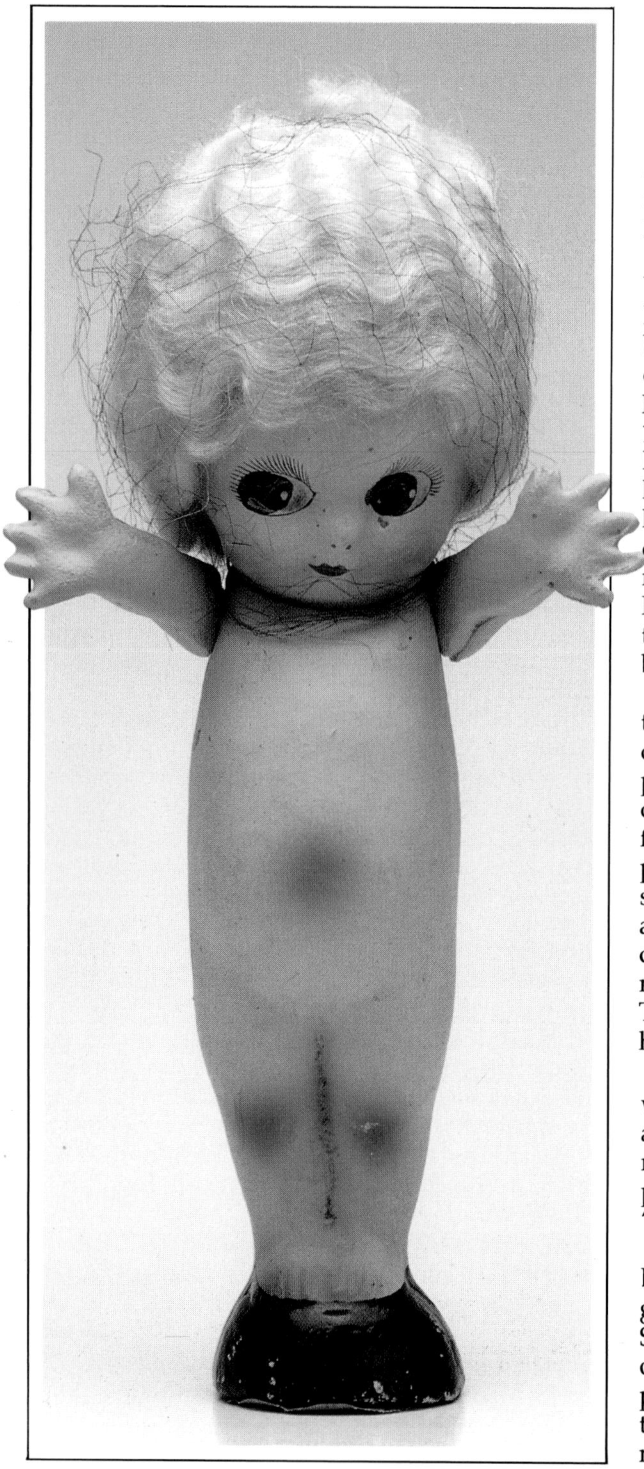

Heinrich Handwerck's factory was founded in 1876 in Gotha, near Waltershausen. Max Handwerck may have been Heinrich's son, and his factory was founded in 1900 for the manufacture of ball-jointed dolls' bodies and dolls' heads. Although it was taken over by Kämmer & Reinhardt it was always run separately. Most of the heads used were manufactured by Simon & Halbig, however, and it is thought that most of the mould numbers ending in '9' are, in fact Simon & Halbig dolls.

Franz Reinhardt was the businessman of the company and after Kämmer died he became much more adventurous and aggressive in his approach. He purchased the Heinrich Handwerck factory in 1902 after the death of Heinrich; this company had been producing dolls' bodies. The Kämmer & Reinhardt dolls made before 1901 were modelled by Kämmer, and after his death they were produced by Simon & Halbig. Indeed the famous Kämmer & Reinhardt character dolls (see page 105) were almost certainly made by Simon & Halbig. Reinhardt expanded and by 1932 his firm had become the leading doll company in Waltershausen, surpassing Kestner. The firm also produced composition, rubber and celluloid dolls made by the Rheinische-Gummi-und-Celluloid-Fabrik Co. with the turtle trade mark. The firm is thought to have introduced the bent-limb baby body — a five-piece body — in about 1909.

Franz Schmidt with the F.S. & Co. of Gengenthal near Waltershausen trade mark came on the doll scene around 1890, making dolls' bodies and parts. Simon & Halbig made heads from his own design and heads are sometimes found with both firms' trade marks. Some of his heads have pierced nostrils or actual holes in the nose: this is said to be his own device and was introduced about 1912. He also made wood, composition and celluloid dolls and he claimed to be the first to manufacture character dolls with sleeping eyes. The first character dolls by Kämmer & Reinhardt had painted eyes.

The firm of Adolf Wislizenus of Waltershausen was one of the earliest companies, dating back to about 1851. He made composition and papier mâché dolls and looked to Simon & Halbig for the production of bisque heads. His heads are marked 'A.W.', 'A.W.W.', 'A.W. Special' and 'Old Glory'.

A few dollmakers were located in neighbouring Bavaria, which was also heavily wooded and has good china clay deposits. One of the best known is Schoenau & Hoffmeister of Burgrub, who began operations in 1901. The firm, which started as a porcelain factory, adopted a five-pointed star trademark. It manufactured open- and closed-mouth dolls, some in regional or 'exotic' costumes.

LEFT *Plaster 'kewpie' type doll with articulated arms, mohair wig, stencilled eyes, painted lashes and a hairnet. (Author's collection.)*

RIGHT *Oriental doll 35 cm/13 in tall, circa 1914 impressed 'F10 243 JDK', with open mouth, blue glass eyes and wearing original Chinese outfit in metal thread, stitched in blues, greens and purples. (Courtesy Sothebys).*

ABOVE *Two painted bisque open-mouth dolls marked 'Armand Marseille, Germany'. Both are in mint condition in their original boxes. The composition, unjointed bodies are 32.5 cm/13 in tall (Collection — Leona and Naomi Gerwat-Clark).*

RIGHT *Bisque-headed open-mouth doll marked K*R, Simon & Halbig 80. She has an open mouth, real hair wig, moulded eyebrows and is 77.5 cm/31 in tall. (Author's collection.)*

OPPOSITE *All-original bisque-headed doll marked 'Armand Marseille A 7½M'. Her clothing is original, though her real hair wig is not. (Author's collection).*

BELOW LEFT *This Armand Marseille doll with an unusual face is marked 'A M 12 Dep Made in Germany'. Her original clothing consists of a green woollen coat and straw bonnet. Her face resembles that of a Heinich Handwerck, and she is pushing a toy baker's delivery cart. (Author's collection).*

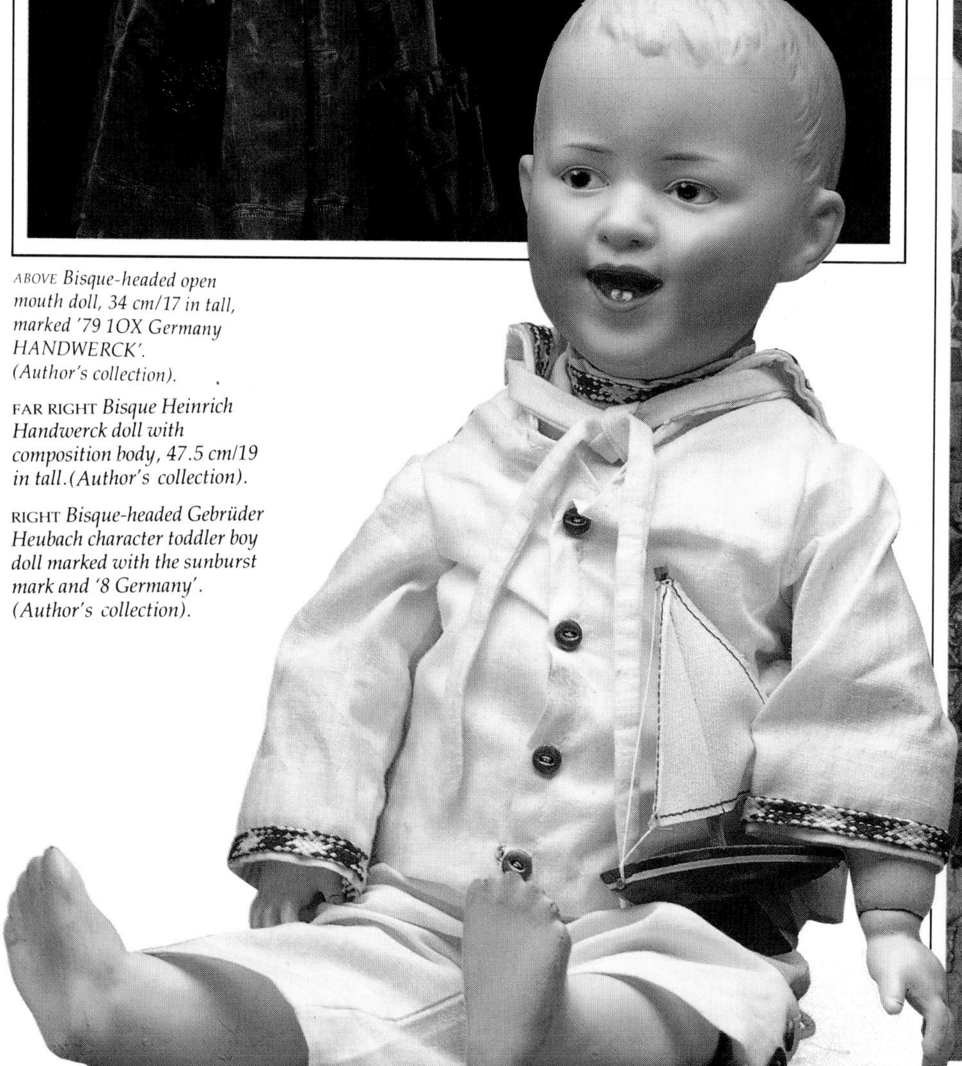

*ABOVE Bisque-headed open mouth doll, 34 cm/17 in tall, marked '79 1OX Germany HANDWERCK'. (Author's collection).*

*FAR RIGHT Bisque Heinrich Handwerck doll with composition body, 47.5 cm/19 in tall. (Author's collection).*

*RIGHT Bisque-headed Gebrüder Heubach character toddler boy doll marked with the sunburst mark and '8 Germany'. (Author's collection).*

## THE CHARACTER DOLLS

The leading dollmakers of Thuringia pioneered the manufacture of the character baby doll. The first such dolls were made by Kämmer & Reinhardt who were said to have been inspired by seeing an exhibition of the dolls by Marion Kaulitz, a 'progressive' designer based in Munich. The decision to make a range of realistic-looking dolls was a move away from the 'dolly-faced' tradition, toward toys with which children could actually identify. It was realised that babies did not usually have very pretty faces, and they looked more like little old men. At first these dolls had an indifferent reception but suddenly their popularity rocketed and the firm had difficulty in meeting the demand. The 1908 slump in the doll world became the boom of 1909. The age of the character doll had arrived. Those produced by Kämmer & Reinhardt were to become the *crême-de-la-crême* of the German doll industry. K & R Character dolls were numbered starting with mould 100. This was superseded by 101 which took the form of a boy or a girl affectionately named Peter or Marie; this model was made with both painted and with glass eyes. Reinhardt's own nephew was used as a model for the boy and girl moulds 114 in 1910, called Hans and Gretchen. This also comes, although rarely, as a head and shoulder plate with a kid body. Some of the model numbers appear to be missing and one can only assume that a few samples were made which were never put into production; for example, 108, 111 and 113 have not come to light so far. One of those to be found is model number 115 with moulded hair, glass eyes, closed mouth and toddler body. Another example, 115a, has a wig, glass eyes, closed mouth, and is the original mould for a Käthe Kruse and a Schoenhut doll. Mould 116 is an older version of 100, the so-called 'Kaiser Baby', a boy with open mouth, teeth and tongue, with painted and moulded hair. This is only a nickname given by collectors to this mould and has nothing to do with the Kaiser as a child; it is thought to be a model of the son of the artist who first sculpted the bust, and in view of the fact that the Kaiser was born in 1859 and the 'Kaiser baby' first made as late as 1908 it is not likely that this particular baby would have been used so many years after his birth. Such are the confusions of the doll world. The next mould is the extremely beautiful 117 in open and closed mouth versions. The 117a open mouth has teeth, and gives an older impression while the 117n, yet another version, has open mouth, teeth and flirting eyes ('n' stands for 'naughty eyes').

That there was some liaison between Kämmer & Reinhardt, Käthe Kruse and Schoenhut dolls is almost certain, but it is possible that ideas were simply copied. At any rate the 115 and 115a

models look exceptionally like Käthe Kruse dolls, and Käthe Kruse modelled her dolls on her own children. Moulds 118–120 have not been found. Mould 121 is a baby or toddler with open mouth, teeth and tongue; 122 a baby or toddler; 123, a 'Funny Face' boy with closed mouth, smiling with flirty eyes; 125 has not been located; 126 is a baby or toddler with open mouth and may be mechanical or with flirting eyes; 127 is a painted-haired baby or toddler boy in bisque; 128–130 have not yet been found. This list shows what an imaginative and innovative company Kämmer & Reinhardt was, and how worthy of the highest accolades in the German doll industry.

Among other makers was the firm of Kestner, whose identifying mould numbers are confusing; sometimes they are accompanied by the initials J.D.K. and sometimes not. Generally speaking, the character mould numbers are in a series from 178–190 (with the exception of 188, which has not been found) and a 200 series. They have open mouths, closed mouths and open/closed mouths (which means that the mouth appears to be open, with parted lips, but the bisque aperture has not been cut). One of the most sought-after Kestner characters is mould 243, the oriental baby.

ABOVE LEFT *Bisque headed shoulder plate doll with open mouth, head marked 'S & H 1079 Dep Germany'. She is 23 inches and has a kid body and wood and composition limbs and original pink lace dress, matching hat and mohair wig. (Granny's Goodies - London).*

ABOVE RIGHT *Simon & Halbig bisque-headed open-mouth oriental character doll 50 cm/20 in tall with head marked 'S H 1129 Dep 10'. Note the delicate colouring. She has a jointed composition body and superb original clothing.*

Armand Marseille made characters with moulded hair, painted eyes and closed mouths with numbers such as 500, 550, 590 and 600. The most famous was the 351 open mouth, or 341 closed mouth, 'dream baby' in various sizes.

Simon & Halbig also made open and closed mouth characters with both painted and glass eyes, with a wide assortment of character numbers, for example 150–153, 1279, 1294, 1299 and some 1300 series numbers, to name a few.

Gebrüder Heubach also made many character dolls. Their numbering system appears to be erratic: those with five-digit numbers would seem to have been the last dolls made, but the 'googlies', which are known to be of a later date, have four-digit numbers. Sometimes the numbers are not impressed properly so care must be taken when interpreting a number. Some dolls have only the sunburst mark and others the square, incised mark. There seems to be no consistency, and one imagines that the confusion must also have affected the manufacturers themselves.

All in all, there was a wealth of character interpretations and the collector certainly has wide scope, even within the products of the Heubach company alone.

ABOVE LEFT *Bisque-headed mulatto doll with open mouth and sleeping eyes. The head is marked 'S & H, K & R'. She has a black, articulated composition body and is 55 cm/22 in tall.*

ABOVE RIGHT *Beautiful bisque-headed doll marked K * R Simon & Halbig 80. She has an open mouth, real hair, moulded eyebrows and a fully-articulated body. She is 77.5 cm/31 in high. (Mildred D. Seeley Collection).*

RIGHT *K * R character doll in mint condition with closed mouth. She is 75 cm/25 in tall and the head is incised 'K * R Simon & Halbig 117'. She has her original dress and underwear, socks and shoes. (Granny's Goodies, London).*

## COLLECTING GERMAN DOLLS – WHERE TO START

**LIMITED BUDGET DOLLS** Many new collectors will start with A & M dolls as these are found most often. The so-called 'dream baby' is a frequent first purchase. The later dolls and baby dolls of the 1910 era made by different manufacturers are also fairly easily found.

**MIDDLE PRICE RANGE DOLLS** The girl dolls made by the well-known Kestner and Simon & Halbig firms would come into this category, condition and face painting being a determining factor regarding price. Originality of costume will also affect price.

**TOP OF THE RANGE DOLLS** Age does not determine price, and the later but rare character dolls are in this group. Rare mould numbers fetch high prices and so do the closed-mouth versions of the girl or 'dolly faced' dolls.

# FRENCH DOLLS

The story of the French doll really begins in the middle of the 19th century. Before that, the influence of the French doll industry was minimal; there were some papier mâché dolls resembling the Sonneberg dolls from Germany, and some German heads on French bodies, but information about them is disjointed and unreliable, and as the heads are unmarked, attribution is difficult. Sometimes it is assumed that a head which is not of the well-known and authenticated German variety, must be either French, or a German head designed for the French market. Generally, there is little evidence to support this.

French dolls in their day were for the pampered rich and, with their exquisite costumes lavishly made in humble back streets by independent outworkers, they have kept their exalted position at the top end of the doll-collecting world to this day. It is this quality, detail and lavishness of costume for which French dolls were perhaps best known; in effect they were complete replicas of the fashions of the day, and today they are highly prized by collectors if they still have their original clothes. It seems astonishing that in 1855 a doll complete with nine-piece layette could be purchased for 1 Franc 19 centimes.

At the roots of development of the French doll industry was the firm of Jumeau, which formed life-blood and gave the impetus to the early French doll industry. Much valuable information has been put together from studies of contemporary exhibition reports and commercial directories without which our knowledge would be sparse. The firm was founded in 1842 by Pierre François Jumeau, who was in partnership with one Belton for a short time; little is known of this person. Early shoulder plate dolls with leather bodies and domed bisque heads are often known as 'Belton heads' though Jumeau claimed that his patent for 'Bébé' dolls had been taken out as early as 1840. The Jumeau factory address appears to have been 18, rue Mauconseil, Paris, until 1867. Emile Jumeau, the younger son of Pierre François, took over the business in 1875 and further developed it. He obtained some heads from Germany, evidently for cheapness, and even bought wax heads from England. His early dolls are marked E.J. for Emile Jumeau and collectors refer to them as E.J.s. In 1873, the firm expanded to factory premises, large

ABOVE *Bisque-headed, closed-mouth French doll 65 cm/26 in high. The head is marked 'F.G. 10' incised in a scroll. She has fixed blue eyes and chubby cheeks and a composition jointed body with fixed wrists. The wig is not original. (Granny's Goodies, London).*

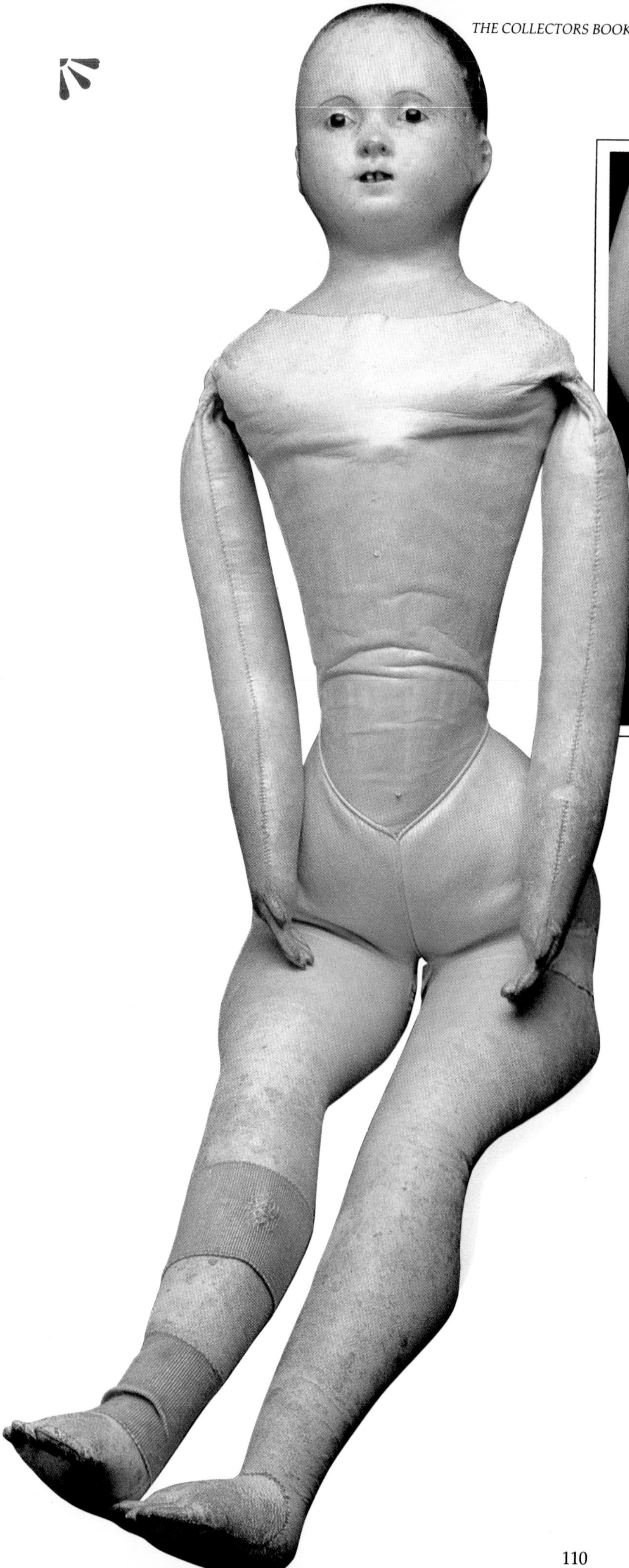

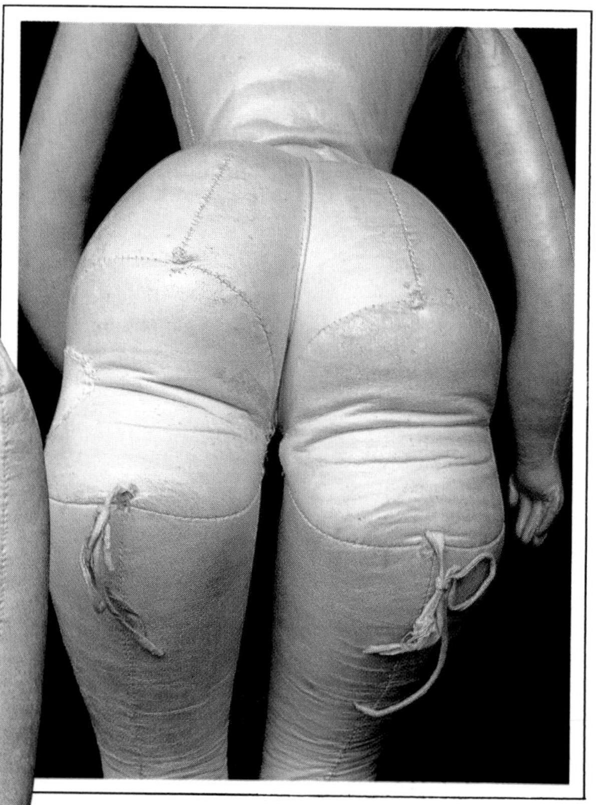

ABOVE AND LEFT *French pink kid body, exquisitely shaped with adult figure and gusset to allow some movement. This type of body was introduced in the mid-19th century. Note the finely-detailed fingers and toes.*

RIGHT *Beautiful Steiner 'A' mould French bisque doll with closed mouth and original clothing.*

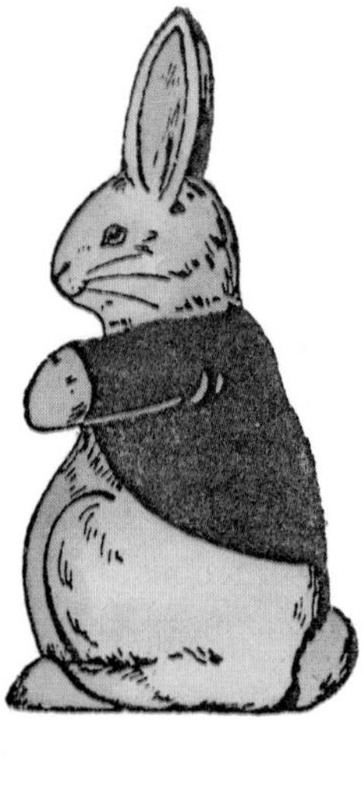

by the standards of the time, in the doll-making area of Montreuil near Paris, but large numbers of outworkers were still used. The building actually exists to this day, but is now owned by a plastics concern. Outworkers were mainly used to design and create the wonderful clothes. Jumeau employed orphans and prisoners — the cheapest available labour force — in an attempt to cut costs; the competition from the cheaper imported German dolls was a constant threat. The quality of the German dolls was excellent, and the German bodies have endured rather better than the French in many cases. The gesso covering on the French bodies tends to be much more brittle and has a tendency to lift off, particularly on the fingers. Pierre François was conservative in his ideas and the success and progress of the Jumeau factory was a direct result of Emile's endeavours. The term 'Bébé' first appears to have been used around 1859 and was in general use by 1870. It was introduced to distinguish those dolls with child-like faces from the dolls representing fashion models, which had the faces of adult women, which are usually referred to as 'Parisiennes'.

## PARISIENNES

Authenticating and dating the early Jumeau heads is extremely difficult since they are unmarked. Parisiennes were developed around the 1860s and were a true creation of their elegant and affluent time. Much as Princess Diana inspires fashions today, the Empress Eugenie inspired many of the luxurious fashions seen on Parisiennes whose original clothing has survived. Often the costume is worn and threadbare, but the collector is urged to be a purist and let repair, rather than replacement, be the general rule. The Parisiennes, with their bustles and fine dresses of silk, taffeta, wool and lace, are a wonderful record of the elegance and extravagance of a bygone time. Parisienne heads were generally attached to a gusseted, stuffed leather body. The limbs are of leather, wood or porcelain. Cheaper heads were made in one piece with the shoulder plate and in these the eyes would sometimes be painted. The wigs were usually of animal fur. Heads are generally unmarked, and the painted-eye variety are often attributed to Huret or Rohmer, though some were undoubtedly made by Jumeau. It can be frustrating for the collector not to be able to identify so many of the Parisiennes. If they are marked, the dolls of the mid-1860s will bear a J.

ABOVE LEFT *Bisque, closed-mouth French bébé doll with brown eyes and head marked 'déposée tête Jumeau Bte. S.G.D.G.' and incised '11'. The body is jointed composition. (Granny's Goodies, London).*

LEFT *Extremely unusual French clown doll with open mouth and, bisque head. The head is incised 'Déposée, fabrication française favorite No. 6 [next word illegible], A.L. & Cie, Limoges' and in red 'Déposée la Géorgienne'. He has a jointed composition body, is 47.5 cm/19 in tall and probably wears original clothing. (Granny's Goodies, London).*

RIGHT *Bisque closed-mouth French bébé doll with brown eyes and head marked 'Déposée tête Jumeau. There are also red tick marks and an incised '9'. The wig and clothing are original. (Granny's Goodies, London).*

## BÉBÉ JUMEAU

The bébés, as mentioned, were the child-like dolls. Their charm was that they could be articulated; early examples have fixed wrists and ball-jointed bodies with separate ball joints at shoulder, elbow, thigh and knee. They were hugely popular and sales soared. In 1881 they were said to have sold 85,000 dolls. By 1889 the firm of Jumeau claimed to have 1,000 employees and to be selling 300,000 dolls per week. The very early dolls were unmarked and are referred to as 'almond-eyed', 'first period Jumeau' or 'portrait Jumeau'. Also from the early period we have the 'Jumeau triste' or, the

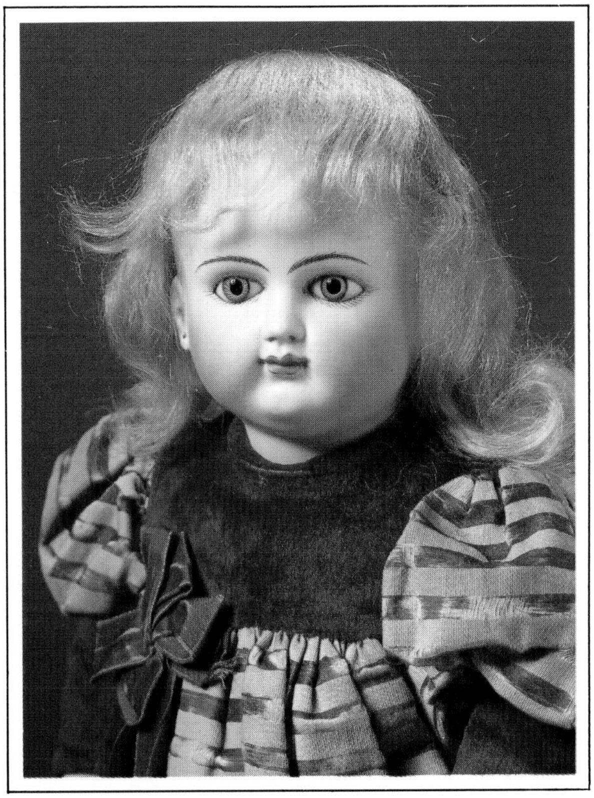

OPPOSITE *Three fashion dolls with bisque swivel heads. From left to right: Jumeau c. 1870 impressed '1', 38 cm/15 in; F.G. doll c. 1880, impressed 'F.G.6' on the shoulder-plate and head, 57 cm/22½ in. The doll in the maroon dress is impressed 'L. déposée 1d' on the shoulder plate and is 37 cm/14½ in high (Courtesy Sotheby's, London).*

ABOVE *This A.T. doll, marked 'A.11.T' has mismatched brows. Her mouth has a light line between the lips. The wig style is similar to old Bru wigs (Mildred D. Seeley Collection).*

ABOVE RIGHT *Early Schmitt doll 42.5 cm/17 in high. The head is marked with crossed hammers in a shield. The wig and clothing are original. (Mildred D. Seeley Collection).*

'Long Face Jumeau', as American collectors call it. These heads are never marked and the bodies bear the *Jumeau Medaille d'Or Paris* stamp in blue. The later closed-mouth Jumeaux are sometimes marked in red *Déposé Tête Jumeau Breveté S.G.D.G.*, sometimes with red and black ticks and check marks, together with a size mark. Others are unmarked except for the size mark, or they bear the ticks and checks together with the size mark. These many also have the oval body label *'Bébé Jumeau Diplôme d'Honneur'*. The *B.L.* mark possibly stands for 'Bébé Louvre', being a doll made by Jumeau exclusively for the Magasins du Louvre department store, between 1880 and 1890. By 1888, the open-mouthed Jumeau Bébé had been introduced. It was more expensive, but nevertheless enthusiastically received. Oddly enough, today the closed-mouth version is twice the price of the open. Some of the open-mouthed dolls are marked with the early closed-mouth red stamp, and all with the size, while others have a simple *Tête Jumeau* stamp in red, and as many again have no mark except the size. There are also those simply marked 1907 plus the size mark.

German competition increased and difficult times came in the mid 1890s. In 1899, the French companies, including Jumeau, banded together under a new title, Société Française de Fabrication de Bébés et Jouets (S.F.B.J.) (French Manufacturers' of Baby Dolls and Toys Company). The group consisted of 10 associates, and although the early

moulds were often used, the quality of the dolls was gradually lost when cost of production became the most important factor. Emile died in 1910 but he lives on though his bébé dolls with their warmth, yet singular aloofness. Some other notable French dollmakers of the period should be mentioned here. They include: Maison Rohmer (1857-1880), E. Denamur, Paris (1857-1898, maker of the Bambin bébé), Schmitt & Fils, Paris (1863-1891), Roullet & Decamps (1865-1910), Fleischman & Bloedel of Fürth, Bavaria and Paris (1873-1914, makers of the Eden bébé), Jullien Jeune, Paris (1875-1904), A. Thuillier, Paris (1875-1890), Petit & Dumontier (1878-1890, makers of 'unbreakable' dolls), Danel & Cie (1889-1895, apparently acquired by Jumeau in 1896, makers of the Paris bébé), and May Frères (1890-1897, also known as May & Bertin and May Fils, who merged with Steiner after 1897, and made the Bébé Mascotte).

ABOVE LEFT *This delightful long-face Jumeau is wearing a handmade original costume, though there is a large bow at the back which may have been added later. (Mildred D. Seeley Collection.)*

ABOVE RIGHT *Beautiful French bisque doll with brown eyes, delicate face painting and original blond mohair wig. Her head is incised 'Bru Jne. 9' and she is also incised on her shoulder plate. She has a swivel neck, kid body, bisque lower arms and wooden lower legs. (Granny's Goodies, London).*

RIGHT *French character doll with blue sleeping eyes, the head marked 'S.F.B.J. 251'. He is 50 cm/20 in tall and is dressed as a sailor boy.*

WELLINGTON
I'm A
TEDDY
BEAR
Booster
Sacramento
84

## BRU (BRU JNR. & CIE, 1866-1899)

Of all the French companies of the period that founded by Leon Casimir Bru in 1866 is at the forefront for quality and innovative design. The firm was continued by his son, Casimir Bru Jeune. Bru dolls have pink or white kid bodies and articulated porcelain or wooden limbs. He made heads of porcelain, rubber or hardened paste, two-faced dolls, and a nursing bébé called Bébé Têteur. The heads on the leather bodies were swivel-necked with bust-shaped breast plates. Early Bru dolls were marked with an incised half crescent and dot, or a circle and dot. These dolls are now among the most prized in any collection and command high prices. Their faces have a whimsical charm surpassed by none and, together with Thuillier ('A.T.') dolls, they stand in the ranks of the top-priced dolls. Later Brus had open mouths and composition bodies. Paul Girard was Casimir Bru's successor in the firm and his dolls were marked P.G.

## GAULTHIER (GAUTHIER) 1860-1916

Fernand Gaulthier was a maker of fine quality bisque-headed fashion dolls on leather or composition bodies. Swivel-neck shoulder plate heads were set on French fashion bodies with kid or bisque arms. They were often marked on the shoulder plate with the initials F.G. and the size. The early girl-doll heads on composition bodies are marked F.G. with the size at the top of the head, while the later mark is the F.G. in a scroll. Dolls were made with both closed and open mouths and were noted for their excellent quality and exceptional eyes: large and piercing, they reach to the very soul of the beholder. The girl dolls have a certain childlike quality, with chubby cheeks.

## JULES NICHOLAS STEINER 1855-1891

Steiners are among the best-loved French dolls, particularly the 'A' mould Steiners with their sweet, expressive faces. The firm acquired the May Frères dolls business in 1897 and specialized in talking mechanical bébés: in 1890 it patented the Bébé Premier Pas (Baby First Step), with open mouth, two rows of teeth and wind-up kid body. This was unmarked and had a domed head as well as a talking mechanism. Steiner won many awards for his dolls. Steiners marked with the 'A' and the size are referred to as 'A' moulds and those with a 'C' and the size as 'C' moulds. The name 'Bourgrin' is found on many of these heads. Some are marked 'Le Petit Parisien Bébé' (The little Parisien baby). 'D' mould and an 'FA' and 'FC' series is also recorded. At the end of the firm's history E. Daspres was running the business.

FAR LEFT *Albert Marque doll 55 cm/222 in tall in original wig and clothing. These are among the finest dolls a collector can own. (Mildred D. Seeley Collection).*

LEFT *French open-closed mouth doll 67.5 cm/27 in tall, incised 'Bru Jne. 11'. Her lips are slightly parted and painted in two colours. (Mildred D. Seeley Collection).*

## COLLECTING FRENCH DOLLS – WHERE TO BEGIN

**LIMITED BUDGET DOLLS** While most French dolls do not fall into this category there is a wealth of S.F.B.J.s to be found as well as tourist dolls. Restored or damaged examples of the better French dolls should be considered, but prices should reflect the extent of damage.

**MIDDLE PRICE RANGE DOLLS** Dolls with open mouths are less expensive than those with closed mouths. Most of the S.F.B.J. character and girl dolls fall into this category, and so do the later examples of the better makes.

**TOP OF THE PRICE RANGE DOLLS** This range includes closed-mouth dolls by any maker, the more popular makes commanding higher prices. The most expensive are Bru, Thuillier ('A.T.'), A. Marque and H. dolls.

ABOVE LEFT *S.F.B.J. (Société française de fabrication de bébés et jouets) character doll with open-closed mouth and head marked S.F.B.J. 236. This is the socalled 'Laughing Jumeau' character doll with two moulded teeth and jointed toddler body, 55 cm/22 in high. (Granny's Goodies - London).*

ABOVE RIGHT *Very rare life-sized French shop mannequin, unmarked but possibly by Bru, with fixed blue eyes, closed mouth and delicate face painting. She has original wig and clothing. (Collection Claude Detave - Paris).*

# THE ERA OF THE MODERN DOLL

ABOVE *Four post-war English dolls. The doll on the right with the blond mohair braids is made of cloth. Next to her is a Pedigree composition bent limb baby with sleeping eyes and a badly-crazed face. The other two are 'pot head' dolls with bent limb bodies (Author's Collection).*

It is difficult to define the modern period for doll manufacture. Madame Alexander, Lenci and Steiff are still in production and their modern creations are much collected, particularly by the young. Such firms as Arranbee were in operation in the USA from 1922 until the 1960s. Mattel Inc.'s 'Barbie' and 'Ken' are a source of renewed interest for the modern doll and bring us into the age of hard plastics and vinyl. Dewees Cochran of California are modern manufacturers of latex dolls, signed under the arm or behind the ear. The Ideal Novelty & Toy Co. of Brooklyn (1907) is another well-known American name. Under the guidance of Benjamin Michtom, whose father, Morris, popularized the teddy bear, Ideal has had much success. Michtom specialized in 'purpose' dolls and linked them with advertisements for certain products. As well as product dolls, Ideal have made well-known characters such as Judy Garland, Snow White, Deanna Durbin and Pinocchio. EFFanBEE is the trademark of another well-known American doll manufacturer, Fleischaker & Baum.

OVERLEAF *Cabbage Patch Kids. These cloth dolls were first launched in 1984 by the American firm of Caleco, Inc. and became the best-selling product in the history of toymaking. Nevertheless, the early models with their own 'adoption papers' are collectors' items. (Caleco, Inc.)*

This firm started in 1912, producing such favourites as 'Baby Grumpy', 'Lovums', 'Skippy', 'Lamkin', and the 'American Children' series of 1939. It also made historical dolls, portrait dolls (1940) and EFFanBEE Limited Edition Dolls (1975).

Peggy Nisbet of Somerset, England has become a specialist innovator in the art of the costume doll with such characters as Henry VIII and his wives, Mary Poppins, Christopher Robin and Pooh Bear. More recently, she produced a limited edition of 1000 Prince Charles and Princess Diana wedding dolls, a limited edition set of 'Royal Children' (Princess Diana with Prince William and Prince Harry) and a royal wedding collectors' limited edition set in hard styrene of Prince Andrew and Sarah Ferguson (The Duke and Duchess of York).

Pedigree Dolls and Toys Ltd, (1938) of Canterbury, England, is another well-known English modern doll manufacturer. This was the first firm in England to make high-quality composition dolls. Among its products were period miniatures (1959) and story book dolls. Perhaps it is best known today for the Sindy doll, first produced in 1962, a 29cm (11½") high teenage doll with a wonderful array of accessories. Barbie and Sindy were launched at the same time, because they were the first modern fashion dolls. Sindy was the first doll to be promoted in television advertisements. The doll became fully posable. Sindy had a monopoly of the British market until 1980.

Pallitoy, another big English manufacturer, brought out the popular 'Tiny Tears' crying and wetting doll in the 1950s.

Dolls are not only playthings for the comfort,

warmth and entertainment of children, but ongoing records of our traditions and way of life.

However, the doll success story of the century is the Cabbage Patch doll, which has had record breaking sales.

A new generation of doll artists is at work producing its own interpretations of our world. The American Doll Artists Association has high standards and guidelines in this respect, as does the British Doll Artists Association. Other creative people are making their own reproductions of old dolls from kits and moulds and this has become a fast-growing hobby, combining history, craftsmanship and a love of dolls to provide highly satisfying personal creations.

I have mentioned modern dolls, not so much in conclusion of the doll story, but to point to a new beginning, for they are tomorrow's collectables, if not already today's. The mechanical gimmicks of the future will be light years away from those wonderful innovations loved by yesterday's children: the age of the microchip and the computer may revolutionize future doll collecting, but what materials will be used is hard to imagine. We have already trodden a long road to Palitoy's 'Tiny Tears' or Mattel's 'Cheerful Tearful' with its changing expressions. Many of today's children find it hard to relate to yesterday's playthings just as the children of tomorrow are unlikely to relate to the toys of today. It is left to the collector to bridge the generations so that tomorrow's children may at least have an awareness and understanding of their past through the things that earlier generations loved.

# RESOURCES

## BIBLIOGRAPHY


Hillier, Mary & T K Pollock's *Dictionary of English Dolls* (London, 1982)
Foulke, Jan *Kestner King of Dollmakers* (USA, 1982)
Foulke, Jan *Gebrüder Heubach Dolls* (USA, 1980)
Hillier, Mary *Dolls and Dollmakers* (London, 1968)
Foulke, Jan *Simon & Halbig Dolls — The Artful Aspect* (USA, 1984)
St. George, Eleanor *The Dolls of Yesterday* (USA 1948)
Coleman, Dorothy *The Collector's Encyclopedia of Dolls* (London, 1968)
Rustam, Phillis A. *Cloth Dolls — A Collector's Guide* (England, 1980)
Buchholz, Shirley *A Century of Celluloid Dolls* (USA, 1983)
Coleman, Dorothy S. *Lenci Dolls* (USA 1977)
Borger, Mona *Chinas — Dolls for Study and Admiration* (USA, 1983)
Hillier, Mary *Automata & Mechanical Toys* (England 1976)
Gerken, Jo Elizabeth *Wonderful Dolls of Papier Mâché* (USA, 1970)
King, Constance Eileen *Jumeau* (England, 1983)
Richter, Lydia *The Beloved Käthe Kruse Dolls Yesterday and Today* (USA, 1983)
Noble, John *Dolls* (USA, 1967)
Eaton, Faith *Dolls in Colour* (England, 1975)
Brecht, Ursula *Kostbare Puppen* (Germany, 1980)
Seeley, Mildred and Vernon, *How to Collect French Bébé Dolls.* (USA, 1985)


## MUSEUMS

### ENGLAND

The Bowes Museum, Barnard Castle, Co. Durham
Bath Museum of Costume, Assembly Rooms, Alfred St., Bath
Birmingham City Museums and Art Gallery, Congrave St., Birmingham
Blaise Castle Folk Museum, Henbury, Bristol BS10 7QS
Cambridge and County Folk Museum, Castle St., Cambridge
Bethnal Green Museum of Childhood, Cambridge Heath Rd., London E2
Victoria & Albert Museum, South Kensington, London SW7
Christine's Doll Museum, 4940 E. Speedway, Tucson, AZ 85712
Cotonlandia Museum, P.O. Box 1635, Greenwood, MS 38930
Cupids Bow Doll Museum, 958 Cambridge Ave., Sunnyvale, CA 94087
Diminutive Doll Domain, Box 757, Indian Brook Rd., Greene, NY 13778
Disney Dolls Museum, Grand Lake 'O the Cherokees, Disney, OK 74340
Doll Cabinet & Museum, Star Rt., Box 221, Ferriday, LA 71334
Doll Castle Doll Museum, 37 Belvedere Ave., Washington, NJ 07882
Doll Museum & Trading Post, Highway 30, Legrand, IA 50142
Doll Museum at Anne Le Ceglis, 5000 Calley, Norfolk, VA 23508
Dolls Den & Museum, 406 River Ave., Point Pleasant, Beach, NJ 08742
Dolls in Wonderland, 9 King Street, St. Augustine, FL 32084
1840 Doll House Museum, 196 Whitfield, Guilford, CT 06437
Enchanted World Doll Museum, Sioux Falls, South Dakota
Essie's Doll Museum, Rt. 16, Beech Bend Rd., Bowling Green, KY 42101
Fairbanks Doll Museum, Hall Rd. (off Rt. 131), Sturbridge, MA
Fairhaven Doll Museum, 384 Alden Rd., Fairhaven, MA 02719
Gay 90's Button & Doll Museum, Rt. 1, Box 78, Eureka Springs, AR 72632
Gerwecks Doll Museum, 6299 Dixon Rd., Monroe, MI 48161
Geuther's Doll Museum, 188 N. Main St., Eureka Springs, AR 72632
Old Brown House Doll Museum, 1421 Ave. F, Gothenburg, NE 69138
Playhouse Museum of Old Dolls & Toys, 1201 N. 2nd St., Las Cruces, NM 88005
Poor Doll's Shop Museum, RR 2, Box 58, Syracuse, IN 46567
Society of Memories Doll Museum, 813 N. 2nd St., St. Joseph, MO 64502
Space Farms Zoo & Museum, RFD 6, Box 135, Sussex, NJ 07460
Storybook Museum, 620 Louis St., Kerrville, TX 78028
Thomas County Museum, 1525 W. 4th St., Colby, KS 67701
Time Was Village Museum, Rt. 51, Mendota, IL 61342
Town of Yorktown Museum & Shop, 1974 Commerce St., Yorktown Heights, NY 10598
Toy Museum of Atlanta, 2800 Peachtree Rd., N.E., Atlanta, GA 30305
Treasure House Doll Museum, 1215 W. Will Rogers, Claremore, OK 74017
University Historical Museum, Illinois State University, Normal, IL 61761
Victorian Doll Museum, 4332 Buffalo Rd., Rt. 33, Rochester, NY 14514
Washington Dolls' House Museum, 5236 44th St. NW Washington, DC 20015
Wenham Historical Museum, 132 Main St., Wenham, MA 01984
Yesteryears Doll Museum, Main & Diver Sts., Sandwich, MA 02563

### DEALERS AND FAIRS

Chelsea Lion, c/o Chenil Gallery, 181-183 Kings Road, London SW3, England
Cohen Auctions, P.O. Box 425 - Rtes. 20-22, New Lebanon, NY 12125, USA
Confederate Dollers, P.O. Box 24485, New Orleans, LA 70124, USA
Grannies Goodies, P.O. Box 734, Forest Hill, London SE23, England
Helen Harten, Red Door Antiques, Prescott, AZ 86031, USA
Jackie Kaner, 9420 Reseda Blvd., Northridge, CA 91325, USA
Kimport Dolls, P.O. Box 495, Independence, MO 64051, USA
The London International Antique Dolls, Toys, Miniatures and Teddy Bear Fair, P.O. Box 734, Forest Hill, London SE23, England
Pollock's Toy Museum, 1 Scala St., London W1
The London Toy & Model Museum, Craven Hill, London W2
The Gallery of English Costume, Platt Hall, Rusholme, Manchester

Arreton Manor, Arreton, Newport, Isle of Wight
The Castle Museum, York

### SCOTLAND
The Museum of Childhood, 42 High St., Edinburgh EH1 1TB, Scotland

### WALES
Penrhyn Castle Museum, Bangor
The Welsh Folk Museum, St. Fagan's, Cardiff

### DENMARK
Leggoland Museum, Copenhagen

### FRANCE
Musée Carnavalet, Paris
Musée des Arts Décoratifs, Paris

### WEST GERMANY
Bavarian National Museum, Munich
Germanic National Museum, Kornmarkt 1, Nuremberg

### HOLLAND
Open Air Folk Museum, Arnhem

### MONACO
Musée Nationale, Mme Gallea's Collection, Monte Carlo

### SWEDEN
Swedish Museum, Djurgården, Stockholm

### USA
Adirondack Center Museum, Court St., Elizabeth-town NY 12932
Alfred P. Sloan Museum, 1121 E. Kearsley St., Flint, M1 48503
Anita's Doll Museum & Boutique, 6737 Vesper Ave., Van Nuys, CA 91405
Antique Doll Museum, 1721 Broadway, Galveston, TX
Aunt Lens Doll & Toy Museum, 6 Hamilton Terrace, New York, NY 10031
Brooklyn Children's Museum, 145 Brooklyn Ave., Brooklyn, NY 11213
Cameron's Doll & Carriage Museum, 218 Becker's Lane, Manitou Springs, CO 80829
Camp McKensie Doll Museum, Mudo, SD 57559
Children's Museum, 3000 N. Meridian St., Indianapolis, IN 46206
Children's Museum, 300 Congress St., Boston, MA 02210
Children's Museum, 67 E. Kirbey, Detroit, MI 48202
Good Fairy Doll Museum, 205 Walnut Ave., Cranford, NJ 07016
Heirloom Doll Hospital/Shop/Museum, 416 E. Broadway, Waukesha, WI 53186
Helen Moe Antique Doll Museum, Hwy. 101 and Wellsona Rd., Paso Robles, CA 93446
Hobby Horse Doll/Toy Museum, 5310 Junius, Dallas, TX 78214
Homosassa Doll Museum, Rt. 5, Box 145, Homosassa, FL 32646
Jacksonville Doll Museum, 5th & California St., Jacksonville, OR 97530
Jonaires Doll & Toy Museum, Rt. 4, Box 4476, Stroudsburg, PA 18360
Lolly's Doll & Toy Museum, 225 Magazine St., Galena, IL 61036
Madame Alexander's Doll Museum, 711 S. 3rd Ave., Chatsworth, GA 30705
Margaret Woodbury Strong Museum, 1 Manhattan Square, Rochester, NY 14607
McCurdy Historical Doll Museum, 246 N. 100 East, Provo. UT 84601
Memory Lane Doll & Toy Museum, Old Mystic Village, Mystic, CT 06355
Mary Merritt Doll Museum, Rt. 2, Douglassville, PA 19518
Museum of Antique Dolls, 505 E. President St., Savannah, GA 31401
Museum of Collectable Dolls, 1117 S. Florida Ave., Lakeland, FL 33803

### PUBLICATIONS
British Doll Artists' Directory, c/o Ann Parker, 67 Victoria Drive, Bognor Regis, West Sussex PO21 2TD, England

Dolls — the Collector's Magazine

Granny's Goodies International Club — Doll World Information Service (send sase for reply), P.O. Box 734, Forest Hill, London SE23, England
Doll Talk, Kimport Dolls, P.O. Box 495, Independence, MO 64071

# INDEX

Page numbers in *italic* refer to illustrations and captions.